C0-AYH-688

An Inquiry into Narrative Deception and Its Uses in Fielding's *Tom Jones*

American University Studies

Series IV
English Language and Literature
Vol. 150

PETER LANG
New York • San Francisco • Bern • Baltimore
Frankfurt am Main • Berlin • Wien • Paris

J. F. Smith

An Inquiry into Narrative Deception and Its Uses in Fielding's *Tom Jones*

PETER LANG
New York • San Francisco • Bern • Baltimore
Frankfurt am Main • Berlin • Wien • Paris

Library of Congress Cataloging-in-Publication Data

Smith, J. F. (James F.)
  An inquiry into narrative deception and its uses in Fielding's
Tom Jones / J. F. Smith.
    p. cm. — (American university studies. Series IV, English
language and literature; vol. 150)
  Includes bibliographical references and index.
    1. Fielding, Henry, 1707-1754. History of Tom Jones.   2. Deception
in literature.   3. Narration (Rhetoric).   4. Rhetoric—1500-1800.
I. Title.   II. Series.
PR3454.H7S6   1993   823'.5—dc20   92-16206
ISBN 0-8204-1941-9   CIP
ISSN 0741-0700

Die Deutsche Bibliothek-CIP-Einheitsaufnahme

Smith, J. F.:
An inquiry into narrative deception and its uses in Fielding's
Tom Jones / J. F. Smith.—New York; Berlin; Bern; Frankfurt/M.;
Paris; Wien; Lang, 1993
  (American university studies : Ser. 4, English language and
literature ; Vol. 150)
    ISBN 0-8204-1941-9
NE: American university studies/04

The paper in this book meets the guidelines for permanence and
durability of the Committee on Production Guidelines for
Book Longevity of the Council on Library Resources.

© Peter Lang Publishing, Inc., New York 1993

All rights reserved.
Reprint or reproduction, even partially, in all forms such as microfilm,
xerography, microfiche, microcard, offset strictly prohibited.

Printed in the United States of America.

For
Kathryn

Acknowledgments

Grateful acknowledgment is made to the following for their permission
to reprint published material:

© David Campbell Publishers, Everyman's Library: Excerpts from Henry Fielding, *The History of the Life of the Late Mr. Jonathan Wild*, 1903; New York: Barnes & Noble, 1967. All rights reserved.

University of California Press: Excerpts from Ian Watt, *RISE OF THE NOVEL: STUDIES IN DEFOE, RICHARDSON, AND FIELDING.* Copyright (c) 1957 Ian Watt.

University Press of New England and Oxford University Press: Excerpts from Henry Fielding, *The History of Tom Jones*, edited by Fredson Bowers, copyright Oxford University Press 1975.

University Press of New England and Oxford University Press: Excerpts from Henry Fielding, *Joseph Andrews*, edited by Martin C. Battestin, copyright 1967 by Martin C. Battestin.

Contents

Preface

This inquiry into the narrative method in *Tom Jones* began with my interest in the ironic convolution caused by Fielding's intrusive methods. The narrator of *Tom Jones* is visible to the reader, foregrounded by his own intrusiveness. His comments on the action he depicts, his commentary in the introductory essays, and his continual discussion of the processes of reading, writing, and criticism reveal the narrator's presence, making it obvious that *Tom Jones* is not an unmediated view of things. At the same time, however, the comic plot of *Tom Jones* is predicated upon the hiding of information. The narrator must maintain the secrets surrounding Tom's birth so that he can reveal them at the proper time and place to bring about the requisite resolution traditional to comic plots. Consequently, while, on the one hand, the narrator and the act of narration itself are both foregrounded, on the other, the narrator's visibility to the reader as a narrative presence must function in an extended act of narrative deception.

This ironic situation leads to a number of questions about Fielding's intrusive narrative method. Why is the narrative act foregrounded? Why is the narrator made visible to the reader through intrusions into the fictive world? How is the deception demanded by the design of the plot actually perpetrated? What are the consequences of such an ironic method? The list of questions could be extended, but the important point is that these questions raised by Fielding's intrusive method all indicate that sustained analysis of the rhetoric employed should offer a profitable approach to the text. My method, therefore, has been to develop close readings of significant passages and to exploit the ironic complications that arise from the many parallel passages in the text. Perhaps one of the most surprising results of this method is the number of references any single passage from *Tom Jones* makes to other passages, themes, metaphorical embellishments, etc. from other places in the text. Indeed, in the final analysis, *Tom Jones* is best understood as a comic network of reference and counterreference with each individual element ironically commenting upon the other elements.

Because of my belief that a comic text must contain defamiliarizing devices, I have rejected the conclusions that Fielding's reflexive method of writing fiction is somehow faulty, that his method violates a necessary verisimilitude, or that the apparent contradictions indicate a lack of philosophical sophistication. Rather, I have attempted to develop the position that, as a writer of comic fiction, Fielding was actually quite aware of what he was doing and that the ironic system of cross-references in *Tom Jones* is an important element of his comic art. As a consequence, I contend that Fielding's *Tom Jones* is a text rich in epistemological investigation and philosophical complexity. Indeed, I would argue that ironic convolution is the glory of *Tom Jones* and a major source of the high-spirited comic play.

I would like to express my appreciation to all whose work has aided in the development and extension of my ideas on Fielding's *Tom Jones*. I have, of course, attempted to be as accurate as possible in documenting sources, but often documentation cannot clearly record the complexities of influence. Beyond such formalities, however, I wish to acknowledge my debt to John Preston and Wolfgang Iser, for, early in the process of composition, I found reassurance and direction from Preston's *Created Self* and Iser's *Implied Reader* and *Act of Reading*. On a more personal level, I would like to offer heartfelt thanks to C. Harry Bruder, Albert W. Fields, and Joseph E. Riehl of the English Department at the University of Southwestern Louisiana for their patient and expert instruction during my years there as a graduate student. I am grateful to David Breeden and Michael P. Spikes for the comments they made after reading drafts of this study, and I appreciate the encouragement and assistance that Carol Hall Wiles has given in the tedious task of proofreading. Finally, I must acknowledge that I owe my greatest debt to Kathryn, my wife and colleague. Without her telling criticism, tireless assistance, and enduring patience, the shortcomings of this little inquiry would be far greater than they are.

CHAPTER
1

Narrative Method and the Deceptive Narrator

*And it is precisely here, of course, that the masks of the clown
and the fool (transformed in various ways) come to the aid of
the novelist.*

M. M. Bakhtin

As a "new Province of Writing," Fielding's *The History of Tom Jones: A
Foundling* appears to be an orderly, well-constituted country, a place where,
after a multitude of alarms, confusions, and mistaken identities, good is
rewarded and evil punished in the best fashion of a comic romance. The
readers of *Tom Jones*, however, find themselves in another, far different
country once they perceive the fundamental incongruities between the
orderly, symmetrical plot and the ironic narrator's intrusive voice. Once a
reader recognizes that Fielding's narrator is not a completely reliable friend
but rather a rogue and comic trickster who misleads and entraps his readers,
the formerly neat, closed-ended reading collapses into ironic contradiction.
The circularity of the comic romance disintegrates under the highly charged
irony of the narrative voice and ends, not in completion, but rather in the
dislocation of ironic comedy.[1] More precisely, the closed and self-sufficient
work becomes an open-ended, "insufficient" text.[2] In fact, even on the level
of the plot, the commonly made assertion that Tom returns to the home of
his childhood with a new-found prudence and his newly won wife lacks
substantial support from the textual evidence. The circular movement from
Somersetshire to London and then back again to the West Country is not
completely closed. Tom and Sophia return to live their married existence on

Squire Western's neighboring estate rather than at Paradise Hall from which Tom had been expelled by Mr. Allworthy (2: 981).[3] Indeed, the narrator's resolution of the different complications of his plot involves both the hiding and then the discovery of the various intrigues of Tom's natural mother, Bridget Allworthy, and his half-brother, Blifil, revealing that he only achieves the artful completion of his birth-mystery plot by behaving as if he were an accessory in these intrigues.

This ironic conflict between the narrator's apparent themes and his actual narrative practice is emphasized by his characteristic intrusions into the fictive world of the text. Ironic, sophisticated, and apparently good-natured, Fielding's narrator foregrounds himself by his intrusiveness. He calls attention to himself as an actual character and to his narration as a narrative act, emphasizing both the artificiality of the plot of *Tom Jones* and the fictiveness of his "history." In this particular regard, Ian Watt correctly asserts in *The Rise of the Novel* that Fielding's "selectiveness of vision destroys our belief in the reality of report, or at least diverts our attention from the content of the report to the skill of the reporter."[4] Fielding's *Tom Jones* is, nevertheless, best not read as merely a failed realistic novel, not, in other words, as a bungled "formal realism," but rather as a complex reflexive text that comically questions the validity of the naïve empiricism that Watt's theory of the novel promotes.[5]

Such questions over the generic nature of the novel and the proprieties of narrative in general have made the history of the critical discussion of Fielding's narrative methods long and contentious. In *Of the Origin and Progress of Language* (1773–1792), James Burnett, Lord Monboddo, anticipated Ian Watt by nearly two hundred years, arguing that Fielding's intrusive narrative method is "not proper for such a work" because it "destroys the probability of the narrative."[6] More recently, Ford Madox Ford complained that Fielding did not care if readers believed in the reality of his characters, and E. M. Forster designated Fielding's intrusive method as "bar-parlour chattiness."[7] With *The Rise of the Novel*, of course, Ian Watt's insistence that the defining characteristic of the novel as a genre is "formal realism" logically entails his criticism of Fielding's method.[8]

In contrast to such negative readings, however, there has developed a second movement in critical thought that increasingly centered on Fielding's narrative method for more positive reasons. Henry James, for instance, wrote with appreciation that Fielding's "fine old moralism, fine old humour and fine old style" all work together and "somehow really enlarge, make every one and every thing important."[9] In "The Plot of *Tom Jones*," R. S. Crane describes Fielding's intrusive narrator as a rather mixed value with regard to the entire textual context. He asserts that Fielding's narrator, "though it is well he should intrude, perhaps intrudes too much in a purely ornamental way." Furthermore, Crane recognizes a slight degree of formal value in the introductory essays when he claims that, although the introductory chapters to each book "serve only occasionally the function of chorus," nevertheless, "we should not like to lose them from the canon of Fielding's writings...."[10]

Continuing and improving upon such tentative moves, Wayne C. Booth conceives of the relationship between "Fielding-as-narrator" and the reader as formulating a "sub-plot" to the narration of Tom's adventures that develops with "no complications, not even any sequence except the gradually increasing familiarity and intimacy leading to farewell."[11] Significantly, Booth places the rhetorical justification for Fielding's highly intrusive narrative method in "the effect of our intimacy on our attitude toward the book as a whole."[12] Developing Booth's position while enriching his own argument with a cue taken from the *Spectator* and the conventions of the periodical essay, Thomas Lockwood argues that "*Tom Jones* presents itself not only as a story, of course, but also as an irrepressible volume of talk."[13] For Lockwood, indeed, this "irrepressible volume of talk" becomes "the larger, more prepossessing book of Henry Fielding's mind and conversation."[14]

This movement from the conception of the narrative act as the means by which the story comes to life expressed by Henry James toward Lockwood's understanding of the story as essentially a subject upon which the narrative voice can perform reflects a dissatisfaction in critical discourse with Watt's "formal realism" or with what Henry Knight Miller terms the "novel credo of bourgeois realism."[15] It further parallels the development of various forms of analysis based on Saussurean linguistics and the general move toward post-modernism. Ironically, such a move constitutes something of a return to both critical methods and a critical awareness of language that are both more sensitive to Fielding's complex art and more productive when applied to his rhetoric than Watt's dictates of "formal realism."[16]

Working on the assumptions that, in contrast to poetic language, language in the novel functions referentially rather than reflexively, as well as that "the genre itself works by exhaustive presentation rather than by elegant concentration," Watt had to denounce Fielding's reflexive narrative method to be logically consistent.[17] An intrusive narrator does indeed destroy the illusion of realism by forcing the reader's attention on the *telling* of the tale rather than on what is *told*. Nevertheless, a theory of the novel founded on "formal realism" cannot productively accommodate a long prose fiction that presents a picture of the life of particular characters living in a particular time and occupying a particular place while also calling attention to itself as a verbal artifact.

A reflexive text questions the transparency of naïve realism by revealing itself as a verbal artifact to the reader.[18] To use a term from the Russian Formalists, it *defamiliarizes* the processes of selection, organization, and interpretation entailed in the plotting of any story by making these various rhetorical processes visible.[19] Fielding's *Tom Jones*, in particular, engages the reader because of the narrator's continual discussion of his narrative method and theory of fiction. Its highly organized, artificial plot and its consistent pattern of diametrically opposed characters reveal that *Tom Jones* is not an unmediated view of things but rather a highly constructed rhetorical creation filtered through an individual human consciousness.[20] The reader engages with the narrative voice in something of the same manner that readers engage with one of Defoe's first-person narrators or with the different "authors" in Richardson's epistolary method. In fact, because of his intrusive character, Fielding's narrator in *Tom Jones* becomes a character, and the act that makes him "known" to his readers is his reflexive narrative act.[21]

Concentrating in particular on Fielding's pervasive use of irony, a number of critics have studied how the narrative voice in *Tom Jones* involves the reader. Eleanor Hutchens, in her study of Fielding's use of irony in *Tom*

Jones, comments that one method Fielding uses to enhance the ironic effect "is to leave the reader to plot a sequence for himself."[22] For Hutchens, Fielding's "reversal of truth and expectation accompanies plot and theme as a sort of ironic *doppelgänger*."[23] She concentrates on local ironies, however, and does not delve into the larger irony of the plot as a whole. At least, she does not develop the manner in which the full dimensions of the "ironic *doppelgänger*" become visible only after the reader has completed an initial reading, only after, that is, the narrator reveals the secret of Tom's birth by producing the hidden text of Bridget's letter that had been purloined by Blifil.

John Preston, on the other hand, deals with exactly this act of narrative entrapment. In *The Created Self: The Reader's Role in Eighteenth-Century Fiction*, he argues that *Tom Jones* must be read at least twice to be fully understood because of the "dual response which secures the ironic structure of the plot."[24] Furthermore, Preston asserts that the active entrapment of readers by the reversal of the plot reforms their judgment by forcing them to see their human limitations and, consequently, directs them toward judging "with full experience and full sympathy," as well as with a tempering measure of forgiveness.[25] Preston concludes his discussion of *Tom Jones* by arguing that the final lesson is that the whole process is "part of a great comedy."[26] In other words, although Preston assigns considerable importance to the reader's enlightenment initiated by Fielding's plot reversals and his ironic entrapment of careless readers, he, nevertheless, claims the general levity of carnival for Fielding's method, insisting with the Chaucer of *Canterbury Tales* that "men shal nat maken ernest of game."[27]

Preston's interest in the reader's active role during reading also leads him to argue that Fielding has managed "to create a reader wise enough to create the book he reads" through the design of the plot.[28] Indeed, Preston claims that in *Tom Jones* Fielding offers the reader many different opportunities to be a bad reader in the belief that such a trap will lead the reader to learn to read well.[29] This view of the text of *Tom Jones* as an active and deceptive test of the reader's ability logically impels Preston to posit a gap between the historical Henry Fielding and the narrator. He argues that the narrator of *Tom Jones* is an "ironic version of the real author" and that "to pose as a bad writer will help Fielding to avoid slipping into shallow rationalism."[30] In support of this view, Preston further claims that Fielding would have been aware that he was violating standard neoclassical epic theory as stated by Le Bossu and that Shaftesbury had deplored the "modern" trait of "modern" authors to intrude personally into their narratives in "Advice to an Author."[31] Consequently, Preston correctly concludes that Fielding's method is "a planned flouting of decorum" by which Fielding "aligns himself with the vain, egotistical, 'modern' author, in the manner of Swift, but with a more subtle ironic intention."[32]

The important change in the understanding of Fielding's narrator in *Tom Jones* from Booth's conception of a sub-text of the evenly developing relationship between the narrator and the reader toward a narrator/reader relationship controlled by the narrator's essentially benevolent rhetoric of deception is further pursued by Wolfgang Iser within the context of his larger interest in the reader and the reading process. In *The Implied Reader*, Iser argues that the discourse between reader and narrator functions to control the reader's subjectivity in the production of "the configurative meaning."[33] The "imaginary dialogue [between the author and the reader] refrains from prescribing norms of judgment for the reader, but it continually gives him guidelines as to how he is to view the proceedings."[34] With the narrator's principle of contrast, Iser contends Fielding offers the reader "a key to the narrative" and, consequently, the text guides the reader to construct balanced judgments about human nature in all of its complexity.

Preston and Iser, therefore, both argue that the ironic plot of *Tom Jones* is designed to hang careful readers on the horns of a critical dilemma and, thereby, to force them to enact "the realization of the text" by resolving the contradictions in a higher-level synthesis.[35] But the pervasive irony of Fielding's text makes it resistant to the construction of such a consistent whole that reinforces the possibilities of human judgment. Indeed, the plot of *Tom Jones* subverts such a higher-level synthesis and reveals the limits of human judgment rather than offering a mere corrective. Consequently, *Tom Jones* is most productively read as a comically skeptical inquiry into the limits of human understanding and not merely as a comic discourse on the method.

Fielding achieves his comic subversion by undercutting his narrator and opening a gap between "Fielding," the implied author, and the narrator of *Tom Jones*. To achieve the complex narrative he plans, the narrator must ironically ally himself with several of the more dubious characters during much of the narrative. His birth-mystery plot determines that he must closely maintain the secret of Tom's birth if he is to reveal that secret at the proper time and, thereby, produce the ironic reversal by the "natural Means" he demands of himself (2: 875–76). To perform this rhetorical feat, the narrator is forced by his plot structure to conspire with Bridget and Jenny Jones. As they plot to disguise Bridget's sexual transgression and to manipulate the benevolent Mr. Allworthy into adopting young Tom, so the narrator is forced to disguise the relevant facts of young Tom's birth and to manipulate the reader during, at least, the initial reading of the text. In particular, he misleads the reader by structuring his ironic characterization of Bridget on the conventional type of the comic spinster.[36]

This rhetorical move not only opens the possibilities for rich local ironies in the text but also misdirects the reader during most of the narrative and allows the narrator to hide the facts he must hide if he is to achieve his particular plot. Furthermore, and with darker consequences, the narrator must link himself with Blifil and the lawyer, Mr. Dowling, for to complete his surprise, he must, like Blifil and his confederate, hide Bridget's letter containing her deathbed confession to her brother, Mr. Allworthy. As the narrative reveals the self-interest and various moral shortcomings of these characters, so the revelation of their hypocrisy reveals the narrator's deceptive rhetoric. While Bridget is interested in maintaining her reputation and perhaps even her position at Paradise Hall, the narrator is concerned for his own reputation as a clever teller of a clever tale. If Blifil's cold self-interest makes him, as Allworthy proclaims, "the worst of Villains" (2: 951), then the self-interested narrator is also guilty of a certain roguish villainy himself.[37]

Of course, the complaint can be made that all narratives must withhold information until the proper time and place and, consequently, that *Tom Jones* is no different from any other narrative in this particular regard. A second argument could maintain that, even if the narrator is guilty of a certain degree of rhetorical complicity, nevertheless, his motives are fundamentally benevolent and praiseworthy. His ends, in other words, justify his means. But Fielding did not have to write *Tom Jones* in the exact way that he did write it. He did not have to construct a narrative that foregrounds both the ironic narrator and the narrative process itself with witty introductory essays and a myriad of other, more local intrusions into the fictive world of Tom's particular difficulties. It is the narrator's intrusiveness, indeed, that gives the text its reflexive character and, consequently, functions to make visible the rhetoric by which the narrator entraps the reader during the initial reading.

The question is one of intention, and as such, there will always be room for debate. Nevertheless, clearly Fielding intended to write a comic prose fiction, and surely he intended his narrator to be a comic one. Furthermore, Fielding's previous narrative practice reveals a history of ironic inversion. In *Shamela*, he deconstructs Richardson's *Pamela* by reversing the virtue/vice discourse. Fielding employs an ironic narrator in *Jonathan Wild* whose good/great discourse plays off the texts of the almost legendary status of the historical criminal and the political career of Robert Walpole.[38] *Joseph Andrews*, a text that like *Tom Jones* is built on the comedy of errors implicit in mistaken identity and a birth-mystery, paradoxically inverts, at least in part, both Richardson's *Pamela* and Cibber's *Apology*. With *Tom Jones*, however, there is no obvious external countertext. Although the narrator does differentiate his text from long-winded romances and voluminous newspapers, it appears as if Fielding's practice of ironic inversion has been both complicated and internalized to a degree that he did not achieve in his previous fiction. Nevertheless, the narrator's revelation of Blifil's villainy also reveals the degree to which he has made the reader a butt of the narrative and the manner in which he has, like Blifil, hidden the truth for his own purposes.

The ironic complication of the narrative voice begins immediately with the opening of *Tom Jones*. In chapter 1, book 1, the first introductory essay and, of course, the narrator's introduction to the reader, Fielding's narrator remarks that "true Nature is as difficult to be met with in Authors, as *Bayonne* Ham or *Bologna* Sausage is to be found in the Shops" (1: 32). He places the distinction between the good and the bad, the authentic and the fraudulent, in the author's skill in presenting his subject, "in well dressing it up" (1: 33). Such a metaphorical relationship between the art of cookery and the art of fiction easily follows from the narrator's initial figure that relates an author to a common innkeeper and his introductory essay to the ordinary's Bill of Fare:

> An Author ought to consider himself, not as a Gentleman who gives a private or eleemosynary Treat, but rather as one who keeps a public Ordinary, at which all Persons are welcome for their Money. (1: 31)

This witty reduction of aesthetic activity to the commonplace activities of a publican appears to establish the reader in the commanding position of an independent patron of any particular innkeeper's table or author's novel that happens to meet with the requirements of taste. Yet this apparent position of authority dissipates with the recognition of the ironic control that the narrator continues to maintain in spite of his polite bow to the reader's critical judgment.[39]

Ironically turning the tables on the reader in this first sentence of *Tom Jones*, the narrator comments that an author should not consider himself a private gentleman but "rather as one who keeps a public Ordinary, at which all Persons are welcome for their money" (1: 31). The word *one*, however, is ambiguous. Does *one* refer to *gentleman*, meaning a private individual of means who entertains his friends as guests, or does it refer to a public "gentleman" who only "entertains" for a suitable fee? The second ironic reading seems the more likely because the statement debunks the traditional sense of authorship as a noble profession and does not allow any selfless sense of civic duty or *noblesse oblige*. Instead, this initial dictum conditions the transaction between author and reader on monetary exchange and, consequently, deflates the profession to the dimensions of the Grub Street hack. An author is not, in other words, a disinterested and voluntary servant of the public good but rather the interested producer of goods for sale with only suspect credentials.

This ironic reduction of the profession of authorship in the initial sentence is only the opening gambit performed by the narrator in his introduction to the reader. Although the narrator claims to continue his author/innkeeper metaphor, he actually shifts the figure in his further development by comparing an author to a cook (1: 33).[40] Not only does the quality of his production reside in his "Cookery" rather than in his subject, but the narrator assumes the control that he had apparently surrendered.[41] Consequently, the narrator concludes:

> How pleased therefore will the Reader be to find, that we have, in the following Work, adhered closely to one of the highest Principles of the best Cook which the present Age, or perhaps that of *Helio-gabalus*, hath produced. This great Man, as is well known to all Lovers of polite eating, begins at first by setting plain Things before his hungry Guests, rising afterwards by Degrees, as their Stomachs may be supposed posed to decrease, to the very Quintessence of Sauce and Spices. In like manner, we shall represent Human Nature at first to the keen Appetite of our Reader, in that more plain and simple Manner in which it is found in the Country, and shall hereafter hash and ragoo it with all the high *French* and *Italian* Seasoning of Affectation and Vice which Courts and Cities afford. By these Means, we doubt not but our Reader may be rendered desirous to read on for ever, as the great Person, just above-mentioned, is supposed to have made some Persons eat. (1: 33−34)

Beyond the implied threat that lurks in the narrator's hope of rendering his readers "desirous to read on for ever," as well as in the allusion to the corrupt court of Heliogabalus, the reduction of reading to extravagant feasting marks a distinctly comic incongruity.[42] Although, on the one hand, the passage may be read as an allusion to Lord Bacon's famous advice that, while some books should only be tasted, others should be eaten whole, the comparison between reading and gluttony, one of the Seven Deadly Sins, undercuts the narrator's extended metaphor. Rothstein indicates a second "sinful" implication when he argues that the "Bill of Fare" degrades "to a predictable avidity to gourmandize on scandal."[43] Whether the fault is gluttony, gossip, or some interesting compilation, it would seem that the narrator assumes that he is writing for readers with tainted pallets, who, indeed, need the spice of corruption to peak their interest.

A further significance of the narrator's initial author/cook, text/feast metaphorical complex relates Fielding's narrator to the typical buffoon of classical Greek Middle Comedy.[44] In *The Anatomy of Criticism*, Northrop Frye points out that Middle Comedy "appears to have been very full of food" and that one conventional buffoon type was the cook.[45] Frye describes this type as related to the parasite and "a conventional figure who breaks into comedies to bustle and order about and make long speeches about the mysteries of cooking."[46] He further states that this figure of the clowning cook was something of "a master of ceremonies, a center for the comic mood."[47] Frye's description of this type clearly fits Fielding's narrator, who does bustle and order about while writing essays on the various mysteries of authorial cookery.

Yet there is still another type of ironic undercutting that can be gleaned from the narrator's opening metaphors, and these spring, not from classical history, classical comedy, or Christian tradition, but rather from internal contradictions in *Tom Jones* itself and from the larger context of Fielding's canon. A reader fresh from *Joseph Andrews* would detect a discordant trace in the narrator's initial comparison between authors and innkeepers. More often than not, inns in that text are places of confusion and confidence tricks that have little to do with either the patron's desires or needs. They seem primarily designed to empty pockets in a purely mer-cenary manner. Certainly, the example of the Tow-wouse inn where Joseph recovers from his robbery and beating does little to recommend the charity and good nature of innkeepers. As Parson Adams discovers when he arrives at the inn, Joseph had not "fallen into the most compassionate Hands."[48] Likewise, the narrator's opening remarks recall the good/great discourse in *Jonathan Wild* because the narrator designates the famous cook he wishes to emulate as a "great Man" and a "great Person" (1: 33–34).[49] In *Tom Jones*, the reader quickly comes to inns where the landlords (or more often the landladies) behave dishonestly or, at least, actively participate in the considerable confusion and misdirection. Besides the "Battle of Upton" in chapter 3, book 9, which begins the extended confusion at the inn there, Tom is wounded earlier at another inn during his fight with Ensign Northerton when the Ensign breaks a bottle over his head (1: 376). Later, the landlady helps Northerton to escape, although he is being detained pending charges because of the expected death of Jones from wounds received. In fact, Northerton buys her assistance with fifty pounds that he embezzles from army funds (1: 392), and her monetary self-interest leads her to snub Tom after she learns from him that he carries his little fortune in his pockets (1: 410). At a third inn, the Jacobite landlord, who was known by his neighbors to be a man of very deep insight into obscure things, mistakes Sophia for Jenny Cameron (2: 576–78).

Even the honest Mrs. Whitefield of the famous Bell in Gloucester, a house which the narrator highly recommends to his readers as an excellent inn (1: 430), is brought to act unkindly toward Tom. After her initially favorable impression of Tom, Mrs. Whitefield allows her good opinion to be altered by the stilted evidence given by the Petty-fogger in her conversation with him and the lawyer, Mr. Dowling. Mrs. Whitefield's manner is so changed toward Tom that he decides to leave the Bell immediately and resume his travels (1: 434). In *Tom Jones*, as in the rest of Fielding's canon, inns are clearly locations of confusion and mistaken identity, places of vice and violence, all spiced with a good measure of dishonesty and self-interest.

The narrator himself makes a curious comment on the firmly established convention of hostility between the brotherhood of innkeepers and their guests in relation to the conversation at the Bell between Tom, Mrs. Whitefield, the Petty-fogger, and Dowling:

> As the Conversation of Fellows of this Kind, is of all
> others the most detestable to Men of any Sense, the
> Cloth was no sooner removed than Mr. *Jones* with-
> drew, and a little barbarously left poor Mrs. *Whitefield*
> to do a Pennance, which I have often heard Mr.
> *Timothy Harris*, and other Publicans of good Taste,
> lament as the severest Lot annexed to their Calling,
> namely, that of being obliged to keep Company with
> their Guests. (1: 432)

Because the narrator's initial figure places the author and the reader in a
publican/guest relationship, this comment ironically dislocates the narrator's
reliability and appears to imply that *Tom Jones* is, like the various inns found
within the text, a place of confusion, misdirection, and mistaken identities.
However, a more serious note is sounded, for the narrator's paraphrase of
Mr. Harris, the famous publican of good taste, indicates a certain degree of
hostility between reader and narrator, a theme that the narrator develops in
his continual references to his readers, the reading process, and, of course,
any "little Reptile of a Critic" (2: 525).

The narrator's opening figure in his introduction to the reader that
metaphorically parallels authorship to the arts of innkeeping and to those of
cookery carries one more significance that represents a further comic
undermining of the narrator's trustworthiness by implying that his rhetorical
method is actually sophistic. In Plato's dialogue *Gorgias*, Socrates refutes
Gorgias's sophistic rhetoric by developing an important analogy between his
rhetoric and cookery, calling both rhetoric and cookery false arts and forms
of flattery:

> Well, Gorgias, I think it [Gorgias's rhetoric] is a
> practice, not of a craftsman, but of a guessing, brave
> soul, naturally clever at approaching people; and I
> call the sum of it flattery. I think this practice has
> many other parts too, and cookery is also one of
> them; it seems to be a craft, but on my account

> (*logos*) it isn't a craft, but a knack and procedure. I
> call rhetoric a part of this too, and also cosmetics and
> sophistry—these four parts set over four things.[50]

Socrates develops his contrast between the four true arts of the body and soul—legislation, justice, gymnastics, and medicine—and the four false reflections or imitations produced by flattery—sophistry, rhetoric, cosmetics, and cookery—as a major point in his attack on Gorgias's sophistry.[51]

As Socrates develops his argument, he makes an explicit comparison between rhetoric and cookery: "What I say rhetoric is, then—you've heard it. It corresponds to cookery, doing in the soul what cookery does in the body."[52] This parallel between Gorgias's sophistic rhetoric and cookery labels rhetoric as the false form of justice in relation to the soul, while cookery is flattery's imitation of medicine in relation to the body. Socrates explains that flattery perceived the four true arts of the body and soul and

> divided itself into four impersonating each of these
> parts, and pretends to be what it impersonates; it
> does not care a bit for the best, but lures and
> deceives foolishness with what is pleasantest at the
> moment, making itself seem to be worth most.[53]

In Socrates's view, the conclusion is obvious; rhetoric and cookery both, as forms of flattery, misdirect and deceive, offering only worldly shadows of the two corresponding true arts—justice and medicine.[54]

Furthermore, the *Gorgias* opens with an intricate battle/feast/rhetoric complex that prefigures the cookery/authorship metaphor of the narrator's opening "Bill of Fare" in *Tom Jones*. As the dialogue opens, Callicles, one of Gorgias's young disciples, welcomes Socrates with an ironic greeting that implies a figurative link between debate and warfare: "This is the way they say you ought to join a war and a battle, Socrates." Socrates responds with a question that transforms the debate/warfare comparison to an apparently more peaceful debate/feast analogy: "You mean we've missed the feast, as they say, and we're too late?" Then Callicles counters with an explicit link between feasting and Gorgias's rhetoric: "Yes, and a most elegant feast it was; for Gorgias put on many fine displays for us a little while ago."[55] Clearly, with this opening to the *Gorgias*, Plato achieves a dramatic introduction of the rhetoric/cookery analogy that Socrates develops as he questions Gorgias and his cohorts during the course of the dialogue. The important point here, however, is that the *Gorgias* establishes a classical precedent for the narrator's opening moves in *Tom Jones* that figuratively joins cookery and sophistry in a philosophical and ethical context.

This famous Socratic comparison between sophistic rhetoric and cookery would seem to brand Fielding's narrator a sophist and his narrative merely rhetoric through the logic of allusion. Consequently, the narrator's initial deployment of the cookery metaphor in his famous "Bill of Fare" undermines the conventional reading of the narrator as benevolent, witty, wise, and, most of all, trustworthy, although he does remain comic and consistently ironic. In fact, his ambivalent, ironic voice challenges the reader's powers of judgment and interpretative ingenuity. Apparently good-natured in his ironic play, Fielding's narrator is a trickster, a sophist, a clown, who, like the cook in classical comedy, directs the celebration and brings ironic rejuvenation. His double-dealing delays and misdirects, forcing readers to reveal themselves and their characteristic patterns of thought. The ironic play keeps readers eating the narrator's culinary delights while striving to construct a coherent whole out of the ambiguities and multiple ironies the text offers for consumption. As Richard Keller Simon argues, *Tom Jones* is "an eighteenth-century fun house" or, more precisely, "a text that is a fearful symmetry of mirrors—of repeating, inverting, mocking mirrors—which control plot structure and character development."[56]

Nevertheless, the narrator of *Tom Jones* should not be read as simply an unreliable blackguard whose performance allows careful readers to discover the mask or, to use Rothstein's formulation, as a tyrant who "secretly exploits the interpretative smugness he prompts in us as first-time readers."[57] The entire narrative situation is more complex than either of these two interpretations, for the narrator's sophistry, his hypocrisy, his devious manipulation of his readers are all relieved by the special and thoroughly traditional privileges of the comic. Indeed, the narrator actually warns readers in the title to the first book that he will withhold significant information and immediately offer only what he deems *"necessary or proper."* His theory of narrative selection commented on throughout the text not only differentiates his text from romances and newspapers, but it also signals the reader that interpretative selection is in progress. A story is being organized, plotted, given a rhetorical purpose.

The narrator's direct reference to narrative selection in the introductory chapter to the second book complicates the complex rhetorical movement of the opening "Bill of Fare" by the introduction of ironic parallels. Although the process entails a degree of ironic subversion because of the narrator's previous use of a dubious analogy between his method of narrative selection and the "Registers of the Lottery" (1: 76), his subsequent assertion in the final paragraph of the essay offers a negative image or mirror duplicate of his "Bill of Fare" by shifting from the language of cooks and cookery to that of social contracts and political authority. While the movement in the first introductory essay slips from jovial publican to master and devious backstage manipulator, the final argument of the second essay moves from Hobbes to Locke, from assertions of divine right and absolute monarchy toward claims of disinterested public service and constitutional controls.[58]

After defining his "new Province of Writing" as a history and setting forth his anti-Richardsonian theory of narrative selection, the narrator proclaims his rights and privileges as absolute sovereign over his narrative domain and, consequently, his reader:

> My Reader then is not to be surprised, if in the
> Course of this Work, he shall find some Chapters
> very short, and others altogether as long; some that
> contain only the Time of a single Day, and others
> that comprise Years; in a word, if my History some-
> times seems to stand still, and sometimes to fly. For
> all which I shall not look on myself as accountable to
> any Court of Critical Jurisdiction whatever: For as I
> am, in reality, the Founder of a new Province of

> Writing, so I am at liberty to make what Laws I
> please therein. (1: 77)

Recalling the allusion in the narrator's opening "Bill of Fare" to the corrupt court of Heliogabalus and foreshadowing Tom's own subsequent meeting with his "*Egyptian* Majesty," King of the Gypsies, in chapter 12, book 12, the narrator appears to claim imperial rights with this declaration.

Nevertheless, the narrator's imperial tone quickly modulates toward the conciliatory voice of benevolent constitutional monarchy:

> And these Laws, my Readers, whom I consider as my
> Subjects, are bound to believe in and to obey; with
> which that they may readily and chearfully comply, I
> do hereby assure them that I shall principally regard
> their Ease and Advantage in all such Institutions: For
> I do not, like a *jure divino* Tyrant, imagine that they
> are my Slaves or my Commodity. I am, indeed, set
> over them for their own Good only, and was created
> for their Use, and not they for mine. Nor do I
> doubt, while I make their Interest the great Rule of
> my Writing, they will unanimously concur in support-
> ing my Dignity, and in rendering me all the Honour
> I shall deserve or desire. (1: 77–78)

The *noblesse oblige* absent from the initial travesty of authorship as commercial cookery is argued here with echoes of legal documentation. A social contract constitutes the legal foundations of the narrator's new province in narrative, and his rights and privileges flow, not from above, not from a grant of divine right, but rather from below, from the reader's recognition that the narrator has performed his task and done his duty well.

Unless *Tom Jones* is to be seen as merely a jumble of local effects, the narrator's shifting arguments, his contradictory positions, must somehow be regulated to a larger dialectical pattern. The paradoxical technique of reflection and refraction creates a profound sense of comic ambiguity that, in its turn, forces readers constantly to restructure their assessment of the narrator's character, as well as his report of the actions of Tom, Sophia, and all of the other characters, actions, and relationships in the text. Forced by the complexities of ironic duplication, readers must continually reassess, a process that undermines any sense of judgmental security. The narrator's revelation of the hidden text of Bridget's letter ultimately reveals the rigidity of the habitual paradigms through which readers have read the text.

This method of narrative testing, which Fielding developed and extended from his dramatic methods of farce and burlesque after the Licensing Act forced him from the stage, reaches its fulfillment in *Tom Jones*, for in *Tom Jones* the dialectic is internalized. Unlike *Shamela* and *Jonathan Wild*, for instance, the countertext is no longer largely external. Instead of satirically contrasting Shamela's "vartue" with Pamela's virtue, the contradictory implications arise from within the narrative voice itself. They spring from the tension between the narrator's playful knavery and the narrative he tells, from the central fact that to reveal the hypocrisy of Blifil (at least in the manner that he goes about revealing it) the narrator of *Tom Jones* must himself become a hypocrite.

Various critics have commented upon the presence of dialectical play in *Tom Jones*. Empson, for example, describes Fielding's narrative method as "double irony," and Harrison views it as "planes and mirrors of transposed points of view."[59] Paulson, in his turn, correctly contrasts the methods of Richardson and Fielding as "one of plenitude" and "one of opposites and larger reference."[60] He maintains that, while Richardson creates "verisimilitude by oppressive intimacy," Fielding's narrative method works "by polarizing his views of people, his kinds of people, and their experiences and motives," and, consequently, Fielding offers "reality as a placing of something in a proper, true relationship to everything else" in contrast to Richardson's "exposition of the authenticity of something."[61] Richardson's substantive technique, in other words, presents a world that he takes to be a transparent copy of "reality." Fielding's, on the other hand, offers, not a world *per se*, but rather an ironic system of relationships that defines through context and dialectical contrast.

Fielding's relational method, however, emphasizes the internalized contradictions in the narration, for, although the narrator assumes an omniscient or transcendental position in relation to the characters in the world of the novel, his relationship with the reader is a first-person one because of his intrusive characteristics. As he narrates his history of Tom's adventures and ultimate success, he also narrates and, therefore, reveals himself as a result of the forced manipulation he must perform to achieve the appearance of a coherent and unified resolution of the plot. Not simply to maintain the necessary suspense (for such suspense is largely relieved by the conventional expectation of the happy comic resolution), but to achieve his particular plot, the narrator must maintain the central mystery of Tom's birth.[62] This mystery is the keystone of the plot structure. Only by intentionally obscuring the facts surrounding Tom's origin and his discovery in Mr. Allworthy's bed can the narrator construct the comic plot of *Tom Jones* as it is constructed. The narrator must willingly conspire with Tom's natural mother, Bridget, and her accomplice, Jenny Jones. He is required to hide Bridget's letter with Blifil.

To be sure, the motivation of the characters and the narrator differs. As Blifil and Bridget are guilty, with differing degrees of culpability, of deceiving Allworthy, so too is the narrator's guilt in deceiving his readers different from that of the characters because of the comic atmosphere in which he performs. Nevertheless, his deception is necessitated by his retrospective narration and his assumption of omniscience. By being guilty of a playful hypocrisy in his act of revealing the more sinister culpability of his characters, the narrator employs a narrative method that dislocates the possibility of a coherent and final reading that centers the apparently providential nature of the comic resolution. Readings such as those generated by Henry Knight Miller and Martin C. Battestin have their major failing in exactly this irony.

Reading through the lexicon of romance conventions, Miller argues that Fielding's *Tom Jones* "cannot be adequately interpreted—or 'decoded'—unless the conventions of romance be adequately interpreted...."[63] Linking Fielding to a past historical milieu rather than to his own and conveniently ignoring the dislocation caused by the New Science and the English Civil War, Miller passes over the subversion of form incorporated into *Tom Jones* and asserts that, although *Joseph Andrews* and *Tom Jones* parody conventions of romance tradition, they "are not in the ultimate sense parodies, any more than Shakespeare's comedies are."[64] Without defining the important distinction between local and "ultimate," Miller adds to this optimistic claim that Fielding had an unqualified belief in the coherent order of things that did not substantially differ from that of the major figures of the English Renaissance:

> Fielding could still vitally and integrally employ the structures and the motifs of romance because he still whole-heartedly believed (with Spenser, Sidney, Shakespeare, *et al.*) in the fundamental cosmic, meta-physical, and social assumptions that had for so long sustained the romance.[65]

For Miller, in short, Fielding is grounded in the "coherent" past and granted an unconditional license of belief in the order of things that does not account for either the crisis of signification signaled by the narrative method of *Tom Jones* or for the historical effects of the hundred and fifty years of civic violence and epistemological upheaval that separate Fielding from the high English Renaissance.

Exploiting a vein similar to that worked by Miller, Martin C. Battestin also strives to ground Fielding in a secure past. Reading *Tom Jones* as "the last and the consummate literary achievement of England's Augustan Age," Battestin argues that, as a man of his age, Fielding was one

> whose cast of mind saw the moral drama of the individual life enacted within a frame of cosmic and social order, conceived in the then still compatible terms of Christian Humanism and Newtonian science, and whose art, conditioned by the principles of neo-Aristotelian aesthetics, saw the poem as fundamentally mimetic of this universal Design.[66]

For Battestin, then, *Tom Jones* "stands as an elaborate paradigm" of an Augustan "belief in the *existence of* Order in the great frame of the universe, and in the *necessity for* Order in the private soul."[67] He locates Fielding's artistic "triumph" in his assumption that *Tom Jones* reflects an official and stable cosmic order in its elements from the grammatical balance of sentence structure to the narrative method.[68] Consequently, "the novel itself is the symbol of its author's universe," and one of Fielding's "chief contributions to the art of the novel" is a "sense of significant design."[69]

Reducing the internal tension of the narrative by grounding Fielding to a secure past and abstracting him from his own particular historical context, Battestin and Miller both overlook the contradictory textual evidence of Fielding's actual ironic "significant design" in *Tom Jones*. By their easy, and convenient, equation of Fielding with his narrator, they reduce the ironic tension between the plot and the narrator's deceptive narrative method.[70] They also overlook the implicit confusion of the signification of good and evil in their insistence that Fielding's "significant design" reproduces cosmic order and the good will of providence in the fictive world, for Fielding's narrator achieves his "providential" resolution of the plot through his ironic narrative tricks. Indeed, the narrator's various rhetorical manipulations reduce the moral distance between himself and the villain of the piece, Blifil.

Consequently, the serious problem of evil in the world of *Tom Jones* as read by Miller and Battestin (as well as others who accept their literary argument from design) can only be solved by arguing that the differences in intention between the characters and the narrator are of considerable moral significance. Blifil's hiding of Bridget's letter, such readers would be forced to argue, is motivated by his own self-interest and viciousness. In regard to the narrator, however, they would be forced to maintain that the narrator's motivation is beneficent, kindly, and, in a word, providential. In other words, their reading would have to assume a certain Machiavellian air: the beneficial ends would justify the dubious means. But, besides ignoring the special conditions and freedoms of comedy, as a symbol of the author's ordered universe, such a situational ethic seems hardly to reflect a serene, untroubled sense of the argument from design and an undisturbed Augustan belief in the essential rightness of things, unless, of course, God himself is to be seen as some sort of an irreverent trickster. In fact, the "significant design" of *Tom Jones* foregrounds the tension between system and history, between the structuring paradigms and the fluid actions structured, by exploiting the tensions between the structured and the structuring voice.

Nonetheless, the argument for such pervasive ironic undercutting in *Tom Jones* could well be pushed too far, and it should not be argued that Fielding either did not or could not have believed in what was essentially a Christian universe. Of course, he did, and his particular brand of Christianity was, as Battestin asserts, Latitudinarian.[71] Still, Fielding's comic mode and his intrusive narrative method create an ironic narrator who deceives the reader throughout the initial reading of *Tom Jones* with his consistent use of narrative trickery. But the narrator is a comic figure, a trickster and rogue, rather than a villain. His sophistic moves force the attentive reader to experience the limitations of human judgment rather than to revel in the complacent assurance of the order of things.

It is for these reasons that the themes of tolerance and mercy are of such importance in the text and why Tom himself illustrates good-heartedness and expounds the rightness of mercy over Allworthy's judgmental objections during the concluding chapters. Tolerance and mercy are necessary in a world where the limits of sound judgment are determined by the limits of knowledge. In such a world, humans can never rest with absolute certainty. Lacking an infallible and transcendental perspective, all they can do is muddle along, constructing flawed judgments with limited knowledge, hopeful guesses, dubious assumptions, and conventional paradigms, fully aware of the ever-present possibility of deception, whether self-inflicted or otherwise. As Fielding asserts in his dedication to *Tom Jones*, his text endeavors "to make good Men wise" by laughing them "out of their favourite Follies" (1: 8), and, indeed, one of most prevalent errors has always been the easy, complacent assumption that one's particular perspective, one's cultural and personal codes, even one's most deeply cherished judgments are all clear and accurate reflections of the overarching order of things in general. Fielding's comic narrator, therefore, deflates this pre-eminent illusion, forcing readers to recognize just how much they do not know whenever they pass judgment on others. Like a wily sophist, or, indeed, like an even wilier Socrates, he conducts his readers through the convolutions of the textual dialogue, until, with a snap, he springs his trap and reveals his secret, evoking joyful laughter at the pervasive extent of human folly and knavery.

WAYNESBURG COLLEGE LIBRARY
93 LOCUST AVENUE
WAYNESBURG, PA 15370

Notes

1. For the range of comic modes, see Northrop Frye, *Anatomy of Criticism: Four Essays* (Princeton: Princeton UP, 1957) 177–86.

2. Robert Scholes contrasts the "boundedness" of the work to the "open, incomplete, insufficient" text:

> As a text, however, a piece of writing must be understood as the product of a person or persons, at a given point in human history, in a given form of discourse, taking its meaning from the interpretative gestures of individual readers using the grammatical, semantic, and cultural codes available to them. A text always echoes other texts, and it is the result of choices that have displaced still other possibilities.

See Robert Scholes, *Semiotics and Interpretation* (New Haven: Yale UP, 1982) 15–16.

3. References to *Tom Jones* are to the Wesleyan Edition and will be cited in the text.

4. Ian Watt, *The Rise of the Novel: Studies in Defoe, Richardson, and Fielding* (Berkeley: U of California P, 1957) 30. For discussion of strengths and weaknesses of Watt's thesis, see Michael McKeon, *The Origins of the English Novel, 1600–1740* (Baltimore: Johns Hopkins UP, 1987) 1–4.

5. Alter defines the "self-conscious novel" as "a novel that systematically flaunts its own condition of artifice and that by so doing probes into the problematic relationship between real-seeming artifice and reality." He sees Fielding's method as a "model for the self-conscious novel." Robert Alter, *Partial Magic: The Novel as a Self-Conscious Genre* (Berkeley: U of California P, 1975) x, xiv.

6. Quoted in Frederic T. Blanchard, *Fielding the Novelist: A Study in Historical Criticism* (New Haven: Yale UP, 1926) 227. For original source, see James Burnett, Lord Monboddo, *Of the Origin and Progress of Language*, vol. 3 (Edinburgh, 1776) 296–98.

7. Ford Madox Ford, *Critical Writings of Ford Madox Ford*, ed. Frank MacShane, Regents Critics Series, gen. ed. Paul A. Olson (Lincoln: U of Nebraska P, 1964) 10–11. E. M. Forster, *Aspects of the Novel* (New York: Harvest, 1955) 82.

8. Watt 32.

9. Henry James, *The Art of the Novel* (New York: Scribner's, 1962) 68.

10. R. S. Crane, "The Plot of *Tom Jones*," *Journal of General Education* 4 (1950): 127.

11. Wayne C. Booth, *The Rhetoric of Fiction*, 2nd ed. (Chicago: U of Chicago P, 1983) 216–17.

12. Booth 216.

13. Thomas Lockwood, "Matter and Reflection in *Tom Jones*," *ELH: A Journal of English History* 45 (1978): 226.

14. Lockwood 226. In the fourth note to "Matter and Reflection," Lockwood expresses some reluctance in using the term *novel*:
> I don't mean that *Tom Jones* ought to be called an essay rather than a novel. "Novel" must continue to be the name for it, I suppose, although I sometimes feel that a more noncommittal term like "book" is better. (235)

15. Henry Knight Miller, *Henry Fielding's* Tom Jones *and the Romance Tradition*, English Literary Studies 6 (Victoria: U of Victoria, 1976) 53.

16. M. H. Abrams defines the critical theory of the neoclassical period as "pragmatic" or "ordered toward the audience." See M. H. Abrams, *The Mirror and the Lamp: Romantic Theory and the Critical Tradition* (London: Oxford UP, 1953) 15–16. Terry Eagleton argues that we should return to a basically rhetorical approach in literary criticism. He maintains that we should "return it [literary criticism] to the ancient paths which it has abandoned." He desires us to examine "the ways discourses are constructed in order to achieve certain effects." Terry Eagleton, *Literary Theory: An Introduction* (Minneapolis: U of Minnesota P, 1983) 205–06.

17. Watt 30.

18. In *The Origins of the English Novel*, Michael McKeon argues that the "romance idealism" of the traditional "aristocratic ideology" was subverted by the empiricism of a "progressive ideology." However, this empirical critique "becomes vulnerable, in turn, to a countercritique that has been generated by its overenthusiasm." McKeon names this countercritique "extreme skepticism" and calls it a new "conservative ideology." He also relates Richardson to the first "progressive" empiricism and Fielding to its dialectical counter, "extreme skepticism" (21–22).

19. Drawing on the well-known Russian Formalist distinction between *fabula* and *syuzhet*, I intend *story* to refer to the raw data that is organized to produce the plot of *Tom Jones*. Consequently, the plot contains not only Tom's story but also the narrator's intrusions and his introductory essays. For definitions of *fabula* and *syuzhet*, see Ann Jefferson, "Russian Formalism," *Modern Literary Theory: A Comparative Introduction*, ed. Ann Jefferson and David Robey (Totowa: Barnes & Noble, 1982) 31. For a criticism of the story/plot distinction, see Barbara Herrnstein Smith, "Narrative Versions, Narrative Theories," *On Narrative*, ed. W. J. T. Mitchell (Chicago: U of Chicago P, 1981): 209–32.

20. See Robert Alter, *Fielding and the Nature of the Novel* (Cambridge: Harvard UP, 1968) 39 and Wolfgang Iser, *The Implied Reader: Patterns of Communication in Prose Fiction from Bunyan to Beckett* (Baltimore: Johns Hopkins UP, 1974) 29–56.

21. Henry K. Miller supposes that "one can argue that Henry Fielding is the 'real' hero of *Tom Jones* without fluttering many dovecotes" because

> We have become accustomed to think of the omniscient (or semi-omniscient) narrator as answering, in some significant respects, the idea of a 'character' in prose fiction, as possessing individual qualities to which the reader responds and which he can assess.

He maintains that in *Tom Jones* "Henry Fielding presented himself as the historical personage Henry Fielding..." and that "Fielding has encapsulated himself within the confines of a literary structure, has made of himself a part of that total aesthetic construct...." See Henry Knight Miller, "Voices of Henry Fielding: Style in *Tom Jones*," *The Augustan Milieu: Essays Presented to Louis A. Landa*, eds. Henry Knight Miller, Eric Rothstein, and G. S. Rousseau (Oxford: Claredon, 1970) 262–66.

22. Eleanor N. Hutchens, *Irony in* Tom Jones (University: U of Alabama P, 1965) 41.

23. Hutchens 67.

24. John Preston, *The Created Self: The Reader's Role in Eighteenth-Century Fiction* (London: Heinemann, 1970) 98.

25. Preston 132.

26. Preston 132.

27. Geoffrey Chaucer, "The Miller's Prologue," *The Works of Geoffrey Chaucer*, ed. F. N. Robinson, 2nd ed. (Boston: Houghton, 1957) 3186.

28. Preston 113.

29. Preston 4.

30. Preston 4, 101.

31. Preston 115–16. Beyond the epic, Fielding's taste for classical history may well have given him another hint. The classical historians also tend to intrude into their narratives with discussions of their methods and the validity of their sources. Two samples, one Greek and one Roman, should illustrate the case:

> I began my history at the very outbreak of the war, in the belief that it was going to be a great war and more worth writing about than any of those which had taken place in the past.

> Most historians have prefaced their work by stressing the importance of the period they propose to deal with; and I may well, at this point, follow their example and declare that I am

now about to tell the story of the most memorable war in
history: that namely, which was fought by Carthage under the
leadership of Hannibal against Rome.

This possible source is supported by the narrator's insistence that he is writing "history."
See Thucydides, *The History of the Peloponnesian War*, trans. Rex Warner (Penguin, 1954)
13 and Livy, *The War with Hannibal: Books XXI–XXX of* The History of Rome from Its
Foundation, trans. Aubrey de Sélincourt, ed. Betty Radice (London: Penguin, 1965) 23.
For an example of Shaftesbury's comments, see Anthony, Earl of Shaftesbury, "Soliloquy
or Advice to An Author," *Characteristics of Men, Manners, Opinions, Times, etc.*, ed. John
M. Robertson, vol. 1 (1900; Gloucester: Peter Smith, 1963) 131–32.

32. Preston 116.

33. Iser, *Implied Reader* 46.

34. Iser, *Implied Reader* 46–47.

35. Iser, *Implied Reader* 35.

36. See Eric Rothstein, "Virtues of Authority in *Tom Jones*," *The Eighteenth Century:
Theory and Interpretation* 28 (1987): 110. For different purposes, Rothstein argues that the
narrator "blinds the reader to the clues of Bridget's maternity."

37. Rothstein argues in "Virtues of Authority" that
the techniques by which Fielding legitimizes his authority lead
to an extension of his irony. His actions as narrator very often
mean more—and often something else—than he says they
mean, with the "more" or "something else" in service to his
self-interest, just as with the characters' actions on which he
slyly comments. And many of his actions function best when
the reader does not really know what they mean. *Tom Jones*,
that is, requires that we accept from Fielding "legitimate"
versions of the same conduct, like deceit, that he prods us to
condemn from the characters. (123–24)
To make his point, he is obliged to equate Fielding and the narrator and limit any ironic
gap between the two. He terms the narrator "reliable" and announces an "axiomatic
assumption that he [the narrator] represents Henry Fielding" (99). Without this identifica-
tion, his argument loses its force. Although the arguments in relation to the narrator's
quest for authority and the power politics he employs may be accurate as a description
of the narrator, they would not apply to the "meaning" of the text if an ironic gap
undercuts the narrator's authority. In the final analysis, Rothstein's argument is useful, but
it fails because he does not fully appreciate Fielding's comic intentions. For a reaction to
Rothstein's argument, see Rex Stamper, "The Narrator of *Tom Jones*: Traditional and
Modern Readers," *Publications of the Mississippi Philological Association* (1989): 197–206.

38. William Robert Irwin, *The Making of* Jonathan Wild: *A Study in the Literary Method*

of Henry Fielding (Hamden: Archon, 1966) 3–42. See also Martin C. Battestin and Ruthe R. Battestin, *Henry Fielding: A Life* (London: Routledge, 1989) 281.

39. Rothstein 107–08. In "Virtues of Authority," he notes this movement from man to master in chapter 1, book 1; however, he neither notes nor discusses its comic contradiction in chapter 2, book 2, where the narrator's argument modulates from absolute tyrant to constitutional monarch.

40. The OED indicates that there was a well-established link between authorship and cookery during the period. Noting the implications of dishonest practice as a figurative meaning of *cookery*, the OED reads: "The action or method of 'cooking' or 'dressing up' (*e.g.* a literary work); the practice of 'cooking' or falsifying...." This meaning is supported by a 1709 quotation from the sixth paragraph of *Tatler* No. 11: "We...have no Occasion for that Art of Cookery, which our Brother Newsmongers so much excel in;...dressing up a second Time for your Tast the same Dish which they gaue you the Day before." This definition is further cross-referenced to the third meaning of *to cook*: "To present in a surreptitiously altered form, for some purpose; to manipulate, 'doctor', falsify, tamper with. *colloq.*" The meaning is supported by a passage from 1636 by Earl Strafforde and a 1751 quotation from Smollett. Clearly, Fielding could have expected his readers to assume the possibility of some sense of falsehood or devious behavior from the use of the authorship/cookery complex.

41. Rothstein 107–08.

42. In *Implied Reader*, Iser relates the narrator's claim that readers can be made to read forever in an attempt to formulate the open-ended definition of human nature offered in *Tom Jones*:

> For in the course of the novel, this ["the representation of human nature"] will always seem to vary according to the background, so that only the technique of contrast can bring to light the hidden sides that inevitably stimulate the reader into trying to discover the identity of human nature. This is why, according to Fielding, the reader will want to read on forever. (49)

The important point here is that the opening "Bill of Fare" indicates that the text is open-ended. The reader can continue to read the text forever because the multiple ironies open the possibilities of many different meanings. Consequently, the text can never be finished or completely consumed, for its irony subverts any reading that oversimplifies the varied complexity.

43. Rothstein 108.

44. Throughout *Henry Fielding: Mask and Feast*, Andrew Wright plays on the relationship between comedy and feasting and the festive. His view of the significance of comedy, however, is too narrow. He tends to see Fielding's comedy as a form of escapism rather than as any more fundamental rejuvenation. In *The Origin of Attic Comedy*, Cornford

indicates the classical relationship between the cook and rejuvenation while discussing Aristophanes's *The Knights*:

> The trade of the Sausage-seller, who is repeatedly called a 'Cook,' has, in fact, been chosen solely in order that he may render this last brilliant service to Demos. We do not need the Scholiast to remind us that Medea more than once performed the same operation of turning an old man into a youth in the flower of his age, by boiling his dismembered limbs in a cauldron.

Consequently, the devious treatment of the reader by Fielding's cook/narrator can be seen as the comedic boiling of the reader in the cauldron of the text to revitalize, replacing the old rigid habits of thought with fresh, flexible ones. See Andrew Wright, *Henry Fielding: Mask and Feast* (Berkeley: U of California P, 1965) and Francis Macdonald Cornford, *The Origin of Attic Comedy* (Gloucester: Peter Smith, 1968) 42. For a detailed study of the tradition of comic rejuvenation, see Mikhail Bakhtin, *Rabelais and His World*, trans. Helene Iswolsky (Cambridge: MIT P, 1968) 1–58.

45. Frye 175.

46. Frye 175.

47. Frye 175.

48. Henry Fielding, *Joseph Andrews*, ed. Martin C. Battestin, *The Wesleyan Edition of the Works of Henry Fielding*, ex. ed. W. B. Coley (Middletown: Wesleyan UP, 1967) 61.

49. In 1752, Fielding defined *great* in "A Modern Glossary" as "Applied to a Thing, signifies Bigness; when to a Man, often Littleness, or meanness." He defined *author* ironically as "A laughing Stock. It means likewise a poor Fellow, and in general an Object of Contempt." See *"A Modern Glossary," Covent-Garden Journal*, ed. Gerard Edward Jensen, vol. 1 (New York: Russell & Russell, 1964) 155–57.

50. Plato, *Gorgias*, trans. Terence Irwin (Oxford: Clarendon, 1979) 463a-63b.

51. Plato 462b–66a.

52. Plato 465d.

53. Plato 464d.

54. George A. Kennedy, *Classical Rhetoric and Its Christian and Secular Tradition from Ancient to Modern Times* (Chapel Hill: U of North Carolina P, 1980) 45–52.

55. Plato 447a.

56. Richard Keller Simon, *The Labyrinth of the Comic: Theory and Practice from Fielding*

to Freud (Tallahassee: Florida State UP, 1985) 73, 11. Treating Fielding in the larger context of comic theory, Simon argues that the narrator is "devious and untrustworthy" and that he "leads the reader on a merry romp through an elegantly symmetrical text of mirrors, inversions and repetitions—a perfect labyrinth" (10). He points out that the "narration is unreliable eccentric storytelling, a masquerade" (60) and that the narrator "is both genius and idiot at the same time" (61). As with Preston and Iser, *Tom Jones* reforms readers for Simon by engaging them: "the novel constantly mocks the reader's wit and judgment. Only by understanding the mockery can the reader learn wit and judgment" (64). Simon argues that Fielding's narrator "is a complex and devious mocker, but the story he has to tell is about a naïve and joyful laugher, Tom Jones" (64).

57. Rothstein 110.

58. Simon argues that, in both *Joseph Andrews* and *Tom Jones,* Fielding creates comic texts that are dialectical conflicts between contrary theories of laughter—the Hobbesian theory of laughter from a sense of superiority and the Shaftesburian theory of laughter from empathy (15).

59. William Empson, "*Tom Jones,*" *Fielding: A Collection of Critical Essays*, ed. Ronald Paulson (Englewood Cliffs: Prentice-Hall, 1962) 124 and Bernard Harrison, *Henry Fielding's* Tom Jones*: The Novelist as Moral Philosopher* (London: Sussex UP, 1975) 45.

60. Ronald Paulson, Introduction, *Fielding: A Collection of Critical Essays*, ed. Ronald Paulson (Englewood Cliffs: Prentice-Hall, 1962) 5.

61. Paulson, Introduction 5.

62. R. S. Crane argues in "The Plot of *Tom Jones*" that the plot of *Tom Jones* creates the effect of "the comic analogue of fear" as the comic replacement of Aristotle's pity and fear (126). The complex comic plot, in other words, does not allow the reader to contemplate seriously Tom's failure or his predicted end on the gallows.

63. Miller, *Romance Tradition* 9.

64. Miller, *Romance Tradition* 20.

65. Miller, *Romance Tradition* 20–21.

66. Martin C. Battestin, *The Providence of Wit: Aspects of Form in Augustan Literature and the Arts* (Oxford: Clarendon, 1974) 141.

67. Battestin, *Providence* 142.

68. Battestin, *Providence* 142.

69. Battestin, *Providence* 142, 147.

70. The narrator in *Tom Jones* claims that Sophia Western most "resembled one whose Image never can depart from my Breast"(1: 156), and this passage is often seen as a reference to Fielding's first wife, Charlotte Cradock, who had died in 1744. Nevertheless, there is surely no necessity to allow a tribute to a deceased wife or those other scattered remarks about known friends and associates of Fielding that appear throughout the text to collapse the ironic gap between the author Fielding and his narrator. To equate Fielding to his narrator is to diminish the ironic richness of the comic text. See Preston 4, 101. For an opposing view, see note 21 above.

71. For the influence of the latitudinarian divines on Fielding, see Martin C. Battestin, *The Moral Basis of Fielding's Art: A Study of* Joseph Andrews (Middleton: Wesleyan UP, 1959). A useful summary of his arguments appears in Martin C. Battestin, Introduction, *Joseph Andrews and Shamela*, ed. Martin C. Battestin (London: Methuen, 1965) v−xl.

CHAPTER
2

Readings of Intrusion and Representation

*One thing, the only truly wise, does not and does consent to be
called by the name of Zeus.*
Heraclitus of Ephesus

Paradoxically Fielding's *Tom Jones* offers its readers a complex comic text
that presents a realistic depiction of particular characters experiencing
important personal events in Georgian England while, at the same time,
systematically working to violate that illusion of reality with a reflexive
narrative method. The narrator's characteristic intrusions, his many discourses
on the method, as well as the ordered, symmetrical plot, all function to
emphasize the narrative act itself and, consequently, the artificiality of the
"History." These devices foreground the fact that the text is a practiced
rhetorical construct, an artifact, and not an unmediated view of the nature
of things. The highly reflexive narrative, however, has inspired considerable
debate about Fielding's exact place in the history of the novel and its rise to
prominence as a genre. Ian Watt, for example, correctly draws an important
distinction between what he neatly terms the "realism of presentation" and
that "of assessment."[1] Maintaining that Fielding helped the fledgling genre
by introducing "a responsible wisdom about human affairs which plays upon
the deeds and the characters of his novels," Watt further claims that Fielding's "realism of assessment" helped to establish the novel as a respectable
genre because "to achieve equality of status with other genres it had to be
brought into contact with the whole tradition of civilised values...."[2] In spite
of granting this historical importance to Fielding's narrative method, Watt

concludes that "Fielding departed too far from formal realism to initiate a viable tradition...."[3]

Beyond proposing a rather narrow definition of the novel, such a mixed appraisal of Fielding's achievement as Watt's fundamentally fails to account for the full range of comic structures that control textual development in *Tom Jones*. Although Watt does not overtly make the case, his final evaluation of Fielding's place in the history of the novel does imply that such a thing as a comic novel is an impossibility because comedy, unlike bourgeois realism, attempts, not to offer an illusion of the world as perceived, but rather to expose the rigidity of habitual modes of action and perception. Comedy, in other words, literally deconstructs: it decenters system to expose limitations and contradictions. Consequently, Fielding's mix of realistic representation and reflexive intrusion is necessitated by his comic intentions. Some technique, some disruptive comic device is needed to dispel the illusion of reality and to create a dual perspective, allowing the comedy of language and circumstance to become visible to readers.

Fielding's intrusive narrator with his introductory essays and local intrusions serves this important comic function. His reflexive method actually reproduces time-honored comic techniques. Classical comedy itself offers the audience a similar mix of grubby realism and highly artificial presentation. Aristophanes, for example, portrays in his various comedies actual individuals, such as Socrates, as well as actions that depict the serious moral and civic consequences of the decay of values in highly fanciful situations. Beyond such dramatic caricatures and the comic masks that apparently caricature actual individuals, the plays themselves are divided by the *Parabasis,* during which the chorus directly addresses the audience, suspending the main action of the drama.[4] Fielding's intrusive method offers a narrative modification of these dramatic devices from Aristophanean Old Comedy. Indeed, his intrusive narrator has long been understood to serve a function similar to the choral commentary in classical drama.[5]

In spite of the classical precedent, Fielding's particular comic mix of realistic and reflexive elements has been used to support radically differing reactions to the mode of representation in his fiction. Historically there have been four major classes of reaction to Fielding's method in *Tom Jones*, and for that matter, in his other fictions as well. On the one hand, some have praised Fielding's realism or "his truth to nature," as an eighteenth-century voice would phrase it. Although these readers might sometimes charge Fielding with moral indiscretion because of his depiction of such actions as Tom's liaison with Lady Bellaston, they finally privilege the perceived realism over moral concerns. Others have denounced Fielding's methods as superficial and conducive to immorality. In many cases, this school of thought has made the representation of characters from the lower levels of society a charge against Fielding, calling his fiction "low."[6] A third group of readers has given qualified praise to Fielding's rhetorical art, while criticizing his intrusive method of narration as a serious violation of verisimilitude, which they consider necessary to the novel. In contrast to this response, a fourth school of thought admits the disruption of the intrusive narrator but maintains that this disruptive voice foregrounds the artificiality of the text for comedic and often epistemological effect.[7]

Representative of the readers who see Fielding as a master of realism, Sir Walter Scott describes Fielding's fiction as characteristically English. He claims that Fielding "made his name immortal as a painter of national manners" through his "extended familiarity with the English character, in every rank and aspect."[8] In spite of the neoclassical theoretical insistence that art should copy "nature," Scott maintains that *Tom Jones*, "the first English novel," made its appearance to a public "which had not yet seen any works of fiction founded upon the plan of painting from nature."[9] As a consequence, Scott also contends that, in contrast to Fielding's novels, Richardson's fictions are modified romances: they "are but a step from the old romance, approaching, indeed, more nearly to the ordinary course of events, but still dealing in improbable incidents."[10]

Nearly one hundred years after Sir Walter Scott argued these views on the value of Fielding's method, Frederic T. Blanchard reiterated his own version of Scott's praise. In the preface to *Fielding the Novelist*, Blanchard claims that Fielding was both the founder and outstanding practitioner of the realistic mode in British fiction:

> Busying itself with what has been said, from year to
> year, of the novelist's work, it [Blanchard's study]
> reveals kinships and antipathies which throw a light
> not merely upon Fielding's genius and achievement
> but upon the development of the *genre* of realism
> which he founded and of which he may be regarded
> as perhaps the most distinguished representative in
> his own country.[11]

Blanchard and Scott, in short, both couple Fielding's reputation as a novelist
to the quality of his realism.

Working under similar assumptions about the novel in their respective
biographies of Fielding, Wilbur L. Cross and F. Homes Dudden both spend
considerable time and effort discussing the different contemporaries that
Fielding could have used as his models for the various characters in *Tom
Jones*.[12] Comparing Fielding's narrative techniques to Garrick's method of
acting and Hogarth's style in painting, Cross argues that, despite "a
heightening of characteristics, restrained burlesque even," Fielding's art
demands that "all characters, all incidents, whatever the recombinations, must
be in harmony with the real world as one observes it."[13] In his turn,
Dudden, citing Lytton as a source for his phrasing, observes that the "flesh-
and-blood vitality" of the characters "immediately strikes us."[14] "They stamp
themselves," he explains, "on the mind as real persons. We believe in them
and are interested in them, just as we believe and are interested in living
people with whom we are familiar."[15]

Such claims that describe Fielding as the father of the realistic novel
in Britain, while sensitive to elements in Fielding's texts, are seriously
misleading, no matter what use Fielding might have made of actual living
persons and identifiable scenes in his composition of *Tom Jones*. Cross, for
example, admits that "the realistic aim in 'Joseph Andrews'—Fielding knew
it as well as his critics—was obscured by his parody of 'Pamela' and his direct
imitation of 'Don Quixote.'"[16] Although Cross does acknowledge in the
parenthetical comment that Fielding was aware of tension between realism
and his own intrusive methods, he maintains that such "secondary aims,

which had led Fielding into exaggeration, burlesque, farce, and some horse-play, were mostly to disappear in 'Tom Jones,' a novel that was to present on a large scale the pure comedy of English life."[17] Following such a logic, Cross finally observes of *Tom Jones*: "The plot was to be artificial; but the characters were to be real men and women."[18]

Neatly rhetorical in the contrast between *artificial* and *real* and also highly ambiguous in the process, such a statement is inadequate for the highly complex and reflexive artificiality of *Tom Jones*. No doubt, Fielding might, in his dedication, have "encouraged the reader to identify Mr. Allworthy with Ralph Allen of Prior Park."[19] Nevertheless, if, as Cross maintains, the details of "the composite scene," of, that is, the prospect and architecture of Mr. Allworthy's Paradise Hall, are indeed a composite figure drawn from the prospect as seen from Tor Hill, the gothic architecture of Radway Grange, and the grounds of Allen's Prior Park, still there can be no real justification for privileging the existence of various models over the artistic composition.[20] Although much in *Tom Jones* might well appear to be "in harmony with the real world as one observes it," there is much that defamiliarizes transparent realism and emphasizes the artificiality of the intellectual pattern imposed upon the material, thereby undercutting the illusion of a clear, transparent view to reality and creating in the reader a sense of play with the various modes and accepted conventions of representing the world. Consequently, realistic depiction is best seen as only one of the many different devices that function within the complex comic reflexivity of *Tom Jones*.

Contrasting such important champions of Fielding's realism as Scott, Cross, and Dudden, another tradition of critical opinion denounces Fielding's method of representation as both low and superficial. Samuel Richardson and Samuel Johnson, two out-spoken members of this school, state their respective cases with considerable vehemence.[21] Writing with notable conde-scension, Richardson argues his case in a letter to Lady Dorothy Bradshaigh, where he reports a comment he had made to Sarah Fielding:

> Poor Fielding! I could not help telling his sister, that
> I was equally surprised at and concerned for his

> continued lowness. Had your brother, said I, been
> born in a stable, or been a runner at a sponging-
> house, we should have thought him a genius, and
> wished he had had the advantage of a liberal educa-
> tion, and of being admitted into good company; but
> it is beyond my conception, that a man of family, and
> who had some learning, and who really is a writer,
> should descend so excessively low, in all his pieces.
> Who can care for any of his people?[22]

For Richardson, Fielding presents sides of life that appear all too earthy and draws characters who remain all too human.[23] Such "low" characters cannot in Richardson's view awaken the vivid concern in the reader that Dudden alludes to in his positive remarks about the attachment raised by their vitality.

Two years after Fielding's death, Richardson once again criticizes the character of Fielding's fiction to Sarah Fielding. In a letter, Richardson reports a critical comment made by a "judge of writing" that slights her brother's knowledge of the human heart in comparison to her own:

> Well might a critical judge of writing say, as he did to
> me, that your late brother's knowledge of it [the
> human heart] was not (fine writer as he was) compar-
> able to your's. His was but as the knowledge of the
> outside of a clock-work machine, while your's was
> that of all the finer springs and movements of the
> inside.[24]

One may well wonder if the "critical judge of writing" was not Dr. Johnson, for the image of the "clock-work machine" that Richardson uses parallels Johnson's famous contrast between characters of nature and those of manners.[25] Still, whether Richardson appropriated Johnson's image or not, the most important point about Richardson's comments to Sarah Fielding is the way they privilege psychology and sentiment over comedy. In this particular regard, Richardson's comments essentially reproduce the widely held and long-standing cultural preference for the serious over the ludicrous, for, in other words, the tragic over the comic, that has been built upon an unfortunate reading of Aristotle's comments on the respective classes of characters depicted by comedy and tragedy in the *Poetics*.[26]

Dr. Johnson's own remarks on the contrasting qualities of Richardson's and Fielding's characterization follow the same pattern as those made by Richardson to Sarah Fielding. In the *Life*, Boswell records Johnson's remark that "there is all the difference in the world between characters of nature and characters of manners; and *there* is the difference between the characters of Fielding and those of Richardson."[27] For Johnson, characters of manners, while "entertaining," are easily understood by "a more superficial observer."[28] Characters of nature, in contrast, are more complex; they are "where a man must dive into the recesses of the human heart."[29] To support his abstractions, Johnson uses the watch analogy that graphically depicts what he sees as the difference between a commonplace reading of the "dial-plate" of manners to a deeper, more substantial knowledge of the inner workings of the human machine:

> In comparing those two writers, he used this expression; 'that there was as great a difference between them as between a man who knew how a watch was made, and a man who could tell the hour by looking on the dial-plate.'[30]

But *nature* and *manners*, the two central terms in Johnson's contrast, can hardly be read as neutral in the light of eighteenth-century critical discourse. *Manners* would imply the particular, the local, the actual streaks of Imlac's individual tulip rather than the universal paradigm. *Nature*, on the other hand, would evoke the critical touchstone of the period, the complex concept that was believed to be, in Pope's formulation, the source, the test, and the end of art. For Johnson, therefore, in order to please many and to please long, any literary composition would have to appeal to and be founded upon nature, and *nature*, as John Dennis defines it, "is nothing but that Rule and Order, and Harmony, which we find in the visible Creation."[31]

Johnson's use of the watch analogy to illustrate his contrast between the characterization of Richardson and that of Fielding figuratively replicates the critical juxtaposition evoked by the manners/nature contrast. As with the two key terms *manners* and *nature*, the watch cannot be understood as being neutral in eighteenth-century terms. The watch and the clock carried much of the conceptual weight of the philosophical argument from design, as well as the entire orderly complex of the Newtonian universal machine throughout much of the period. To assert, therefore, that Richardson knew the inner workings of the watch carries much the same significance as maintaining that he could see into the inherent structure of things and that, like Newton in Halley's famous praise, he was nearer to the gods. Merely to read the dial-plate would only entail a more or less common understanding of the local language and manners, only to be, as it were, literate in the surface effects of civil life rather than to be intimate with the inner springs that propel the entire harmonious machinery of creation.

Johnson's criticism of Fielding's methods of characterization from his perspective of universal paradigms conforms to his moral criticism of the effects of Fielding's fiction on its readers. Boswell records that Johnson called Fielding a "blockhead" and a "barren rascal" whose pictures were "of very low life."[32] Hannah More, in her turn, reports in a letter to her sister that the only time she saw Dr. Johnson angry with her was after she had made a rather flippant allusion to *Tom Jones*. She explains that, after Johnson expressed some shock that she would even acknowledge having read "so vicious a book," he said that he hardly knew a work more corrupt.[33] Beyond such remarks in conversation as these reported by Boswell and More, however, *Rambler* No. 4 marks Johnson's most important statement of what he saw as the central moral shortcoming of the new style of prose fiction of which *Tom Jones* is such a notable example. As the "comedy of romance," these texts attempt to "bring about natural events by easy means, and to keep up curiosity without the help of wonder"; consequently, they

> are such as exhibit life in its true state, diversified
> only by the accidents that daily happen in the world,

and influenced by passions and qualities which are really to be found in conversing with mankind.[34]

Johnson claims that these comic romances, which he maintains were written for "the young, the ignorant, and the idle," may well produce dangerous moral effects by misleading young readers who, lacking fixed principles through inexperience, might well be "open to every false suggestion and partial account."[35]

Developing his concerns, Johnson argues that the potential effects of a close representation of the moral complexities of life mixed with realistic depiction could produce a state of moral confusion in the unwary reader:

> Many writers, for the sake of following nature, so mingle good and bad qualities in their principal personages, that they are both equally conspicuous; and as we accompany them through their adventures with delight, and are led by degrees to interest ourselves in their favour, we lose the abhorrence of their faults, because they do not hinder our pleasure, or, perhaps, regard them with some kindness for being united with so much merit.[36]

In other words, Johnson maintains that the authors of such morally ambiguous fiction corrupt their readers through a kind of Epicurean desensitization to vice. For him, their treatment of the various ambiguities of moral life "confound the colours of right and wrong, and instead of helping to settle their boundaries, mix them with so much art, that no common mind is able to disunite them."[37]

Essentially a clever version of an old and standard complaint of the moralistic, Johnson's argument in *Rambler* No. 4 parallels the confession that he makes in the preface to his dictionary of a latent desire to "embalm" language, forestalling change as a consequence and relieving the tension between the general system and the individual utterances of everyday linguistic practice. Johnson admits in the preface that he had once "flattered" himself with the hope that he could "fix our language, and put a stop to those alterations which time and chance have hitherto been suffered to make in it without opposition."[38]   Still, he reluctantly recants that fond hope, acknowledging that it is not supported by either reason or experience:

> When we see men grow old and die at a certain time
> one after another, from century to century, we laugh
> at the elixir that promises to prolong life to a thou-
> sand years; and with equal justice may the lexicog-
> rapher be derided, who being able to produce no
> example of a nation that has preserved their words
> and phrases from mutability, shall imagine that his
> dictionary can embalm his language, and secure it
> from corruption and decay, that it is in his power to
> change sublunary nature, or clear the world at once
> of folly, vanity, and affectation.[39]

Calm and sensible, Johnson's comments here still infer a certain regret that the corruption of flux cannot be replaced with a steady permanence in life, as well as in language.   The important point, however, is that Johnson links linguistic change to death and decay—an implication made obvious by his use of *embalm* in relation to a lexicographical project.   The fallen, sublunary world ends, in short, in the corruption of both life and language.

Johnson concludes *Rambler* No. 4 with a similar conflict between what he sees as the desirable permanence of paradigms and the corruption of worldly change, although here he expresses his argument in the terminology of linguistics and natural philosophy rather than those of linguistics and natural corruption.   In spite of the slight shift in terminology, Johnson reproduces the profound sense of conflict between the overreaching system and the confusion of everyday practice expressed in his comments from the preface to his dictionary and in his distinction between characters of nature and those of manners.   Johnson's claim that the newly popular comic romances "confound the colours of right and wrong" pivots on the meta-phorical use of *colours.* Alluding to Newton's studies in optics, the phrase implies that to confound right and wrong through a close imitation of everyday life would be analogous to returning the rainbow of the spectrum, refracted by the prism and defined by scientific theory, back to white light, to remix things, as it were, into their undifferentiated "natural" state. At the same time, however, confusing "boundaries" so "that no common mind is able to disunite them" also involves creating a crisis in signification, a crisis in the absolute understanding of *good* and *evil* brought on by a revelation of the inadequacies of moral paradigms to deal with the situational complexity of human life. Johnson's fear of these texts that offer a just copy of the diversity of human action derives from this tension he perceives between moral paradigms and the particular ambiguous actions illustrated. In his view, these mixed texts confuse the reader, blurring clear distinctions. It is with such underlying assumptions that Johnson evokes both optics and language to illustrate his argument about the moral effects of the new fiction on the "common mind" when under the sway of the sublunary world.[40]

So, when Dr. Johnson asserts that he "cannot discover why there should not be exhibited the most perfect idea of virtue; of virtue not angelical, nor above probability, for what we cannot credit we shall never imitate, but of the highest and purest that humanity can reach," he not only privileges Richardson over Fielding, but he also asserts a paradigmatic or, to use Auerbach's term, a "figural" theory of realism.[41] The individual thing or any particular action gains its significance from the degree to which it repeats or recalls some eternal paradigm. For Johnson, the tension between the model and the execution, between the paradigm and the syntax, or the *lange* and the *parole*, must be subsumed in the transcendent model itself; a vertical or paradigmatic reading dominates the horizontal or syntagmatic one. Realism becomes morally useful only insofar at it verifies a particular and universal grammar of things, that is, only insofar as it is, in fact, a philosophical realism. Indeed, it is by no means an accident that Johnson's only extended fiction, *Rasselas*, is a stoic and pessimistic sermon under the guise of an oriental tale.[42]

The criticism of Fielding's methods of representation as being both low and superficial, such as that offered by both Johnson and Richardson, hinges on a specific theory of mimesis and the considerable ambiguity of the word *nature*. To follow nature, to be natural, and all the variant phrases can mean any of several different things. On the one hand, to follow nature might signify making an "iconic" copy of the things of this world as perceived, while, on the other, to be natural can mean imitating certain patterns or structures that are understood to be universal. As M. H. Abrams remarks while discussing the eighteenth-century French theorist Batteux, "This imitation, however, is not of crude everyday reality, but of 'la belle nature'; that is, 'le vrai-semblable,' formed by assembling traits taken from individual things to compose a model possessing 'all the perfection it is able to receive.'"[43] In their criticism, therefore, both Johnson and Richardson attack Fielding's level of representation. Yet Abrams also correctly observes that imitation "did not, in most theories, play the dominant part" in literature, for it was the Horatian dictum of delight and enlightenment that controlled the central rhetorical element of neoclassical theory.[44] Consequently, Johnson's criticism of Fielding's fiction as being morally incorrigible takes precedence in his view over questions of mimesis because an imitation that copies the ambiguous complexities of human life complicates the signification of good and evil by introducing tension between the moral structures and the human processes structured while, at the same time, sweetening the mixture with the pleasures of imitation and rhetoric.

Such considerations of Fielding's methods of representation, both those that praise his "iconic" realism and those that condemn his work as low and superficial, fail to account fully for the important ambiguities in Fielding's method. Later critics, such as Ian Watt in *The Rise of the Novel* and Michael Irwin in *Henry Fielding: The Tentative Realist*, have developed the debate over Fielding's reflexive method by introducing the formal considerations of style and genre.[45] These modern critics were anticipated by nearly two hundred years, however, when Lord Monboddo complained in his *Origin and Progress of Language* of Fielding's use of an intrusive narrator and of the mock-heroic or burlesque passages in *Tom Jones*. Such parodies, Monboddo argues, are "not proper for such a work" because they represent "too great a change of style."[46] He continues by referring specifically to the intrusive method:

> *Secondly*, because it [the parodic intrusion] destroys
> the probability of the narrative, which ought to be
> carefully studied in all works, that, like Mr. Fielding's,
> are imitations of real life and manners, and which,
> accordingly, has been very much laboured by that
> author.... This, therefore, I cannot help thinking a
> blemish, in a work which has otherwise a great deal
> of merit, and which I should have thought perfect of
> the kind, if it had not been for this, and another fault
> that I find to it, namely, the author's appearing too
> much in it himself, who has nothing to do in it at all.
> By this...I mean his reflections with which he begins
> his books, and sometimes his chapters.[47]

Essentially paralleling Ian Watt's claim that "Fielding's stylistic virtues tend
to interfere with his technique as a novelist," Lord Monboddo's early
criticisms of Fielding's intrusive method clearly privilege "the probability of
the narrative" over such comedic concerns as parody and burlesque.[48]

Yet there lurks a paradox hidden in readings that accept the assumptions that underlie the arguments of Lord Monboddo and Ian Watt. Basing
their criticisms on the codes of verisimilitude or "formal realism," they insist
that a novel should appear to be an unmediated or transparent copy of
things as perceived. Ironically, however, an imitation of the world can only
be judged as a good or a bad copy of things if the reader also acknowledges
it to be an imitation. Based ultimately on Aristotle's claims in the *Poetics*
that humans possess an instinctive delight in mimesis and that literary arts
are mimetic, such readings locate a good measure of the aesthetic pleasure
in a recognition of the justness of the copy, and they deal out praise for the
imitator on the same terms.[49] In such a nature/artifice discourse, however,
a novel can only be enjoyed as a novel if it acknowledges its fictiveness in
one way or another. Readings that praise Fielding's realism or those that
condemn his "lowness" do not adequately account for the complexities of the
text. Although Monboddo and Watt acknowledge important traits of Fielding's method, they do not play the complex game of art and artifice that

Fielding has his narrators play in all of his fiction, but most particularly in
Tom Jones, when creating a "nature methodized" that, while containing
elements of realism, also lays bare the acts of writing and reading, of
construction and interpretation.

In contrast to DeFoe and Richardson, who either deny or obscure the
fictiveness of their text, Fielding exploits the artificiality and creates neither
a transparent "iconic" realism nor a "figural" one, but rather a dialectical
game. Readings that concentrate on Fielding's realism, whether in positive
or negative terms, only offer partial readings of the text by being blind to
the comic intentions implicit in the various tensions raised by the intrusive
narrator. Only a reading that acknowledges the uses made of elements of
realism and the defamiliarizing devices that undermine the illusion of
verisimilitude will account for the complexities of Fielding's comic art.

Throughout his fiction, Fielding uses intrusive, reflexive narrators who
plot the events narrated around obviously constructed antithetical characters
and scenes. Indeed, antithetical construction is a hallmark of Fielding's
style.[50] In *Jonathan Wild*, for example, Wild himself and all of his gritty
underworld stand juxtaposed to the Heartfree family and their romance
existence, giving dramatic illustration to the good/great discourse. *Joseph
Andrews* affords numerable examples as Adams, Joseph, and Fanny travel
on the roads between London and the Booby country estates. Adventures,
such as Parson Adams's appeal for funds from the swine-keeping Parson
Trulliber, graphically reproduce the debate between faith and good works.[51]
The antithetical tension remains operative down to the stylistic level.
Trulliber, in a self-righteous heat fired by Adams's assumptions about
Christian charity, proclaims indignantly: "I would have thee know, Friend,
(addressing himself to *Adams*,) I shall not learn my Duty from such as thee;
I know what Charity is, better than to give to Vagabonds," reproducing the
dramatic conflict between knowledge and action in the grammatical balance
of his speech.[52] Knowledge need not lead to action, and rigid faith might
not produce good works.

The most complex text in Fielding's canon, *Tom Jones* incorporates and
improves upon the antithetical give and take of the two earlier efforts.

Commenting upon the uses of the style in *Tom Jones*, Robert Alter asserts that Fielding employs antithesis "not merely to give a pleasing symmetry to his style but to focus satiric meanings with a high degree of concentration."[53] Following this initial claim about Fielding's purpose with an appreciation of Fielding's methods, Alter contends that

> one can see that Fielding belongs with the group of novelists which includes such varied figures as Sterne, Conrad, Proust, Joyce, and Faulkner, for whom style is not just the means of conveying or framing events but, often, the event itself.[54]

Not only is Fielding's narrative method central, as a system of differentiation, to the creation and concentration of meaning, but his method also becomes the significance itself by reproducing in its antithetical constructions the tensions operative in human understanding.[55]

Yet Fielding has his narrator introduce elements that undermine the clear-cut system of definition that Alter implies in his assertion about Fielding's use of antithetical concentration.[56] In the introductory chapter to book 4 of *Tom Jones*, the narrator distinguishes his own "History" from "those idle Romances which are filled with Monsters, the Productions, not of Nature, but of distempered Brains" (1: 150). The narrator also claims that there is an important distinction between his own text and a voluminous history or, to use his own terminology, a "News-Paper of many Volumes" that simply transcribes events without the application of any particular active principle of selection (1: 151). Consequently, he differentiates his own selective construction from that of the dryasdust historian who

> to preserve the Regularity of his Series thinks himself obliged to fill up as much Paper with the Detail of Months and Years in which nothing remarkable happened, as he employs upon those notable Æras when the greatest Scenes have been transacted on the human Stage. (1: 75)

The narrator maintains that he must take "every Occasion of interspersing through the whole sundry Similes, Descriptions, and other kind of poetical Embellishments" (1: 151). For without such stylistic contrasts, "the best Narrative of plain Matter of Fact must overpower every Reader" (1: 151). Only a transcendent perspective, that of "the everlasting Watchfulness, which *Homer* has ascribed only to *Jove* himself," can protect the reader from the tedium of "a News-Paper of many Volumes" (1: 151).

Besides the satiric jab at the voluminous methods of Richardson, these claims made by the narrator in the introductory essay to book 4 qualify each other and create a highly complex dialectical pattern that parallels the systemic use of antithetical characterization, setting, and syntactical structure. As the narrator plays Tom against Blifil, Allworthy against Western, Partridge against Honour, and a vast array of other contrasts, so he places claims of an accurate recording of "plain Matter of Fact" against a reflexive theory of narrative selection complemented by claims of necessary stylistic contrast. With this process, he undermines verisimilitude and foregrounds artificiality.

Such a use of intellectual patterning contradicts those readings that emphasize Fielding's realism. No matter how real may appear the dramatic personnel of *Tom Jones* and the exactness of the complicated time scheme that reportedly controls both Tom's and Sophia's wanderings, the reflexive narrative destroys the voyeuristic illusion of naïve realism.[57] As the narrator argues that "Truth distinguishes our Writings from those idle Romances," he also maintains that unfiltered mimesis would be unbearably dull for both writer and reader (1: 150–51). Consequently, it is not surprising that the narrator would have quoted Pope's famous couplet from the "Essay on Criticism" in his first introductory essay: "True Wit is Nature to Advantage drest, / What oft' was thought, but ne'er so well exprest" (1: 33). For the narrator of *Tom Jones*, meaningful "History" springs from the raw data of the plain matters of everyday life filtered through the selective intelligence of the human structuring agent, not from an unmediated reproduction of events.

Within this context, several of Auerbach's comments in *Mimesis* on the representation of reality are relevant. In the epilogue, Auerbach stresses that he came to see the violation of the classical doctrine of levels of style as central to the rise of modern realism. Writing of the nineteenth-century French realists Stendhal and Balzac, he argues that

> they broke with the classical rule of distinct levels of style, for according to this rule, everyday practical reality could find a place in literature only within a frame of a low or intermediate kind of style, that is to say, as either grotesque comic or pleasant, light, colorful, and elegant entertainment.[58]

He also maintains that the realistic rebellion against the classical doctrine of levels of style could not have been "the first of its kind," and he locates the initial assault in "the story of Christ, with its ruthless mixture of everyday reality and the highest and most sublime tragedy."[59]

The important point here is that Auerbach's argument on the irreconcilable conflict between a self-sufficient realism and a reflexive notion of decorum or levels of style exactly reproduces the tensions that Fielding's narrator insists on to differentiate his "Heroic, Historical, Prosaic Poem" from either romances or newspapers (1: 152). Consequently, Ford Madox Ford's criticism that Fielding does not care if the reader believes in the characters as real, existent individuals is, at least in one sense, correct, while still being remarkably wrong-headed.[60] The wrong-headedness resides, as with Watt's criticism, in a tacit assumption that Fielding should be writing a kind of novel that he is not.[61] Nevertheless, Fielding's narrator sets himself the curious and paradoxical job of being "natural" and violating the appearance of nature through the use of obviously artificial styles.

The radical ambiguity that controls the realistic elements in *Tom Jones* is made patently clear in the prefatory chapter to book 8. Entitled "*A wonderful long Chapter concerning the Marvellous; being much the longest of all our introductory Chapters*," this introductory essay is the single most important text within *Tom Jones* on the question of realism. On the surface, it appears to be a witty, but standard, argument for the Aristotelian principle of probability, replete with documentation and footnotes. Indeed, this chapter has often been used as central evidence in arguments on Fielding's practice and theory. However, this particular introductory essay is built on an irony that continually undercuts the apparent claims made, and, when placed in conjunction with other elements and statements from *Tom Jones*, it reveals a continuation of the comic tension previously indicated in the introduction to book 4.

Ian Watt makes use of the introductory chapter to book 8 as central data in his argument against Fielding's narrative practice. While commenting on Fielding's use of the epic tradition, he observes:

> Fielding, then, prescribed a greater emphasis on verisimilitude for the new genre than that current in epic or romance. He qualified this, however, by admitting that since 'the great art of poetry is to mix truth with fiction, in order to join the credible with the surprising', 'complaisance to the scepticism of the reader' should not be taken to a point at which the only characters or incidents permitted are 'trite, common, or vulgar; such as may happen in every street, or in every house, or which may be met with in the home articles of a newspaper.'[62]

Watt also correctly maintains that "by 'the surprising'" Fielding is "referring primarily to the series of coincidences" that immediately follow as both Tom and Sophia crisscross their respective journeys toward London.[63]   Still, the statement quoted above reveals a flaw in Watt's treatment. The important clause on the art of poetry being the clever mixing of fact and fiction, which Watt takes as a significant admission on Fielding's part, is placed in inverted commas to signal that it is quoted from *Tom Jones*, but Watt does not reveal that this is a quotation that the narrator documents in the text as being from the fifth chapter of *Peri Bathous: or, Martinus Scriblerus, His Treatise of the Art of Sinking in Poetry*.

This particular Scriblerian passage significantly compares a literary text to a labyrinth, and, as Fielding's narrator develops his own argument, so Martinus Scriblerus too moves from a highly ironic discussion of unity of character as represented on the "modern" stage to the general laxity of "modern" morals:

> His design ought to be like a labyrinth, out of which no body can get clear but himself. And since the great Art of all Poetry is to mix Truth with Fiction, in order to join the *Credible* with the *Surprizing*; our author shall produce the Credible, by contradicting common opinion. In the very Manners he will affect the *Marvellous*; he will draw Achilles with the patience of Job; a Prince talking like a Jack-pudding; a maid of honour selling bargains; a footman speaking like a philosopher; and a fine gentleman like a scholar. Whoever is conversant in modern Plays, may make a most noble collection of this kind, and at the same time, form a complete body of *modern Ethics and Morality.*[64]

Taken in its totality, this passage from *Peri Bathous* is clearly one of the literary antecedents of the introductory essay to book 8, and, most certainly, the reader of *Tom Jones* is encouraged by the narrator's documented allusion to the Scriblerian text to anticipate ironic implications in his assertions.

Given Fielding's satiric bent and the fact that he had connected himself with the Scriblerians in his published version of *The Tragedy of Tragedies* by using the persona of Scriblerus Secundus in the parodic notes, it is not surprising that Fielding would once again appeal to the Scriblerians as a subtext to his own irony. As Watt asserts about *Tom Jones*, such "a very neat and entertaining formal structure" does "compromise the narrative's general air of literal authenticity by suggesting the manipulated sequences of literature rather than the ordinary processes of life."[65] But, by ignoring the irony introduced into the passage by the acknowledged source of the claim that poetry mixes fiction and truth, Watt removes the narrator's comments from their context and creates the possibility for his straightforward reading. In fact, the passage quoted from such a questionable source as Martinus

Scriblerus undermines the trustworthiness of the narrator and opens the chapter to multiple ironies—a situation signaled by its cumbersome title.

Yet when the narrator claims that his essay is both long and wonderful, he only introduces the ironic play that culminates in his acknowledgment that the principle that poetry mixes fiction and truth comes from "a Genius of the highest Rank" (1: 406). The phrase is ambiguous. He could be referring to the fictional Scriblerus or to Pope himself. Nonetheless, the quotation comes in the midst of the narrator's summation:

> Within these few Restrictions, I think, every Writer may be permitted to deal as much in the Wonderful as he pleases; nay, if he thus keeps within the Rules of Credibility, the more he can surprize the Reader, the more he will engage his Attention, and the more he will charm him. As a Genius of the highest Rank observes in his 5th Chapter of the *Bathos*, 'The great Art of all Poetry is to mix Truth with Fiction, in order to join the Credible with the Surprizing.'
>
> (1: 406)

The narrator then contradicts Scriblerus's proposal to imitate nature in her lowest forms by rejecting the "trite, common, or vulgar," as well as such events "as happen in every Street, or in every House, or which may be met with in the home Articles of a News-paper" (1: 407). Still there can be no doubt that Fielding intends the quotation to be recognized (at least by the well-read members of his audience) and its context to be applied to the capabilities and character of his narrator.

The narrator himself has already ironically undermined the argument of authority a number of times in the course of his essay. First, he under-cuts both Homer and Pope when discussing the "wanton and extravagant Imagination" of the classical deities:

> This hath been strongly urged in Defence of *Homer's* Miracles; and it is, perhaps, a Defence; not, as Mr.

> *Pope* would have it, because *Ulysses* told a Set of foolish Lies to the *Phæacians*, who were a very dull Nation; but because the Poet himself wrote to Heathens, to whom poetical Fables were Articles of Faith. (1: 397)

The narrator develops this comment by placing two classical authorities in opposition: he wishes "*Homer* could have known the Rule prescribed by *Horace*, to introduce supernatural Agents as seldom as possible" (1: 397–98). Next, the narrator implicates the traditional high seriousness of the epic. He admits that, since the behavior of the immortals in the *Iliad* and the *Odyssey* would "have shocked the Credulity of a pious and sagacious Heathen," he has been "sometimes almost inclined, that this most glorious Poet, as he certainly was, had an Intent to burlesque the superstitious Faith of his own Age and Country" (1: 398).

This ironic jab at the Homeric gods is followed by the repetition of an allusion to Samuel Butler's *Hudibras*. First used in the introductory essay to book 4 (1: 150–51), the allusion deflates poetic inspiration by linking it to intoxication through overindulgence in ale:

> Lord *Shaftesbury* observes, that nothing is more cold than the Invocation of a Muse by a Modern; he might have added that nothing can be more absurd. A modern may with much more Elegance invoke a Ballad, as some have thought *Homer* did, or a Mug of Ale with the Author of *Hudibras*; which latter may perhaps have inspired much more Poetry as well as Prose, than all the Liquors of *Hippocrene* or *Helicon*.
> (1: 398–99)

Here the allusion to Shaftesbury recalls "A Letter Concerning Enthusiasm" and its attack on religious extremism, as well as its call for the test of ridicule.[66] The use of Butler's *Hudibras*, which in book 4, chapter 1, is linked to *Hurlothrumbo*, indicates not only a deflation of inspiration but also

an attack on religious extremes. In its turn, the comic allusion parallels the
previous assault on pagan beliefs in the mock hint on Homeric burlesque
intentions. It seems to be significant that the rejection of invocations in the
modern context counters the arguments that important personages should be
introduced by suitable fanciful writing put forth in the narrator's preface to
book 4. Certainly, this argument on the limitations of the marvelous, with its
rejection of invocations, ironically looks forward to the introductory chapter
of book 13, "*An Invocation*" (2: 683–88).

The web of allusion and contradictory implications is complicated by
the narrator's pretense of forgetfulness:

> It is, I think, the Opinion of *Aristotle*; or if not, it is
> the Opinion of some wise Man, whose Authority will
> be as weighty, when it is as old; 'that it is no Excuse
> for a Poet who relates what is incredible, that the
> thing related is really Matter of Fact.' This may
> perhaps be allowed true with regard to Poetry, but it
> may be thought impracticable to extend it to the
> Historian: For he is obliged to record Matters as he
> finds them; though they may be of so extraordinary
> a Nature, as will require no small Degree of historical
> Faith to swallow them. (1: 400)

The inference that Aristotle's authority as a literary dictator is based as much
on mere age as on veracity pulls the underpinning from both the argument
from authority and the neoclassical doctrine of pleasing many and long in
exactly the same way that the supposed forgetfulness ironically deflates the
narrator's argument of the need for probability. A comic *tour de force*, the
narrator maintains an argument theoretically built on Aristotle's *Poetics* while
pretending only a limited knowledge of that very document, and this pretense
in an essay in which the narrator alludes to M. Dacier, Homer, Pope,
Shaftesbury, Butler, Herodotus, Drelincourt, DeFoe, Clarendon, and others.

The nexus of reference in this chapter becomes even more complex
with the recognition of the echoes to the Ancients and Moderns controversy.

Such allusions are only fitting in an ironic essay constructed upon Aristotle's *Poetics* and a quotation from the *Peri Bathous* of Martinus Scriblerus. Nonetheless, the use of Shaftesbury's contrast between the poetic possibilities of the Ancients and the misguided practices of the Moderns, as well as the undercutting of the theory of authority implied in the narrator's reference to authority and mere age, recalls Scriblerian attacks on "modern" pedantry. It can even be argued that the two allusions respectively take the opposite sides in the debate. While the allusion to Shaftesbury condemns the "modern" practice of writing puerile invocations in the language of a dead religion, the opinion that authority may be based on mere age rather than on veracity can be seen to side with the Moderns.

Consequently, the introductory essay to the eighth book of *Tom Jones* indicates the narrator's highly ironic and ambiguous attitude toward even the Aristotelian argument of probability. While the statement that the "Art of all Poetry is to mix Truth with Fiction" is in and of itself reasonable and parallels the argument of the necessity of "poetic Embellishments" to relieve "plain Matter of Fact" in the fourth book, there is nevertheless a tension between the positions maintained in these two introductory essays. In book 4, the narrator asserts the uses of poetic passages to enhance the dignity of important characters. Here, in the eighth book, the narrator draws a distinction between poetry and history that recalls the poetry/history discourse of the *Poetics*. Although the narrator acknowledges that sometimes facts will stretch the bounds of credulity, he still observes that a historian "is not only justifiable in recording [facts] as they really happened; but indeed would be unpardonable, should he omit or alter them" (1: 401). He does allow for the omission of "other Facts not of such Consequence nor so necessary," such as "that memorable Story of the Ghost of *George Villers*," from *The History of the Rebellion*, but he argues that a historian who tells what happened will "sometimes fall into the Marvellous, but never into the Incredible" (1: 401−02).

By asserting that a poet may omit, although a historian may not, the scarcely credible that is known to have happened and by supporting this claim with such famous events from the past as "the successful Expedition of

Alexander related by *Arrian*" and "the Victory of *Agincourt* obtained by *Harry the Fifth*" (1: 400–01), tension is enhanced. Chapter 1, book 4 demands poetry to relieve the dry narration of facts. It maintains that, without patently artificial human selectiveness and embellishment, mere unprocessed data would remain unreadable. On the other hand, chapter 1, book 8 argues that to maintain the credibility of the reader, to remain in "Complaisance to the Scepticism of a Reader" (1: 401), an author "must keep likewise within the Rules of Probability" (1: 400). To fail to do so "by falling into Fiction" is the time that the historian "forsakes his Character, and commences a Writer of Romances" (1: 402). To maintain credibility is to earn a certain trust from the reader, "who is indeed guilty of critical Infidelity if he disbelieves him" (1: 407).

Two conflicting demands, therefore, are foregrounded in *Tom Jones*. The narrator must avoid "falling into Fiction" in his character of a historian; but, at the same time, he declares with Martinus Scriblerus that the art of poetry is a mixture of fact and fiction. Based on the concerns of audience reaction, such a poetry/history discourse returns once again to Aristotle's *Poetics*, where Aristotle asserts that "poetry is something more philosophic and of graver import than history, since its statements are of the nature rather of universals, whereas those of history are singulars."[67] Ironically, the narrator continually terms himself a historian, although he defines *Tom Jones* as a mixed construction, as, in one of many different constructions, a "Heroic, Historical, Prosaic Poem" (1: 152). It should be noted that in the preface to *The Journal of a Voyage to Lisbon* Fielding maintains his preference for history over poetry.[68] However, in the twelfth number of the *Covent-Garden Journal*, Fielding's Sir Alexander Drawcansir, Knt., asserts with Doctor South that most histories are filled with lies.[69]

In addition, the conflict between the demands of history and those of fiction that the narrator emphasizes with his introductory essays also operates in tensions between the essays and the story proper. In the initial chapter of the eighth book, the narrator contrasts the historian who draws from public events and those authors "who deal in private Character" (1: 402). He argues that examples of evil behavior will always receive more credence than those of the "greatly good and amiable" (1: 402), and he supports his claim with two extended examples (1: 402–04). First, he offers the story of a Mr. Fisher who cold-heartedly murders his friend and patron, Mr. Derby, to whom he "long owed his Bread" (1: 402). Opposed to this exemplum of villainy, follows an extended and elegant compliment to Ralph Allen as an unnamed gentleman who is "charitable to the Poor, and benevolent to all Mankind" (1: 403–04, 403n).

These two examples function as illustrations within an argument for the "Conservation of Character," during which the narrator praises the view of George Lyttelton, "a most excellent Writer," to the effect "That Zeal can no more hurry a Man to act in direct Opposition to itself, than a rapid Stream can carry a Boat against its own Current" (1: 405, 405n). The narrator completes this observation by his own assertion that a man may not act contrary to "the Dictates of his Nature" (1: 405). Curiously enough, this statement appears to be directly contradicted by the introductory chapter to the previous book, book 7.

Reacting to Black George's theft of Tom's money in book 6, the narrator in the introductory chapter to the seventh book, "*A Comparison between the World and the Stage,*" argues a different position:

> A single bad Act no more constitutes a Villain in Life, than a single bad Part on the Stage. The Passions, like the Managers of a Playhouse, often force Men upon Parts, without consulting their Judgement, and sometimes without any Regard to their Talents. Thus the Man, as well as the Player, may condemn what he himself acts; nay, it is common to see Vice sit as awkwardly on some Men, as the Character of *Iago* would on the honest Face of Mr. *William Mills.* (1: 328–29)

Although this passage tends toward the ironic because of the placing of passion over judgment, the narrator follows it with the injunction that a "Man of Candour, and of true Understanding, is never hasty to condemn," for such men will "censure an Imperfection, or even a Vice, without Rage against the guilty Party" (1: 329). Only, in the narrator's judgment, those "worst of Men" often will have "the Words *Rogue* and *Villain* most in their Mouths" (1: 329).

These two moral pronouncements tend toward different understandings of the motive process of human behavior. The statement from the eighth book is the more conventional and simplistic. A man will act in accord with his nature, and strong emotion or "Zeal" will only "hurry" the said man on toward the expression of his nature. The second, more tolerant view from book 7, no doubt designed to catch readers in their harsh judgment of Black George's betrayal of friendship, does not argue for the single, self-contained, even monolithic self that the first does. It proposes a more complex notion of moral action and recognizes the possibilities of a divided self driven by the very complexity of circumstances toward dubious action.

It is of considerable importance that these two opposing theories of moral action can both be applied as interpretations of Tom's own character. A harsh judgment would assert that Tom's many indiscretions reveal not a nature too warm for its own good but rather a thorough corruption. Such a judgment, however, would ally the reader with Thwackum, Square, and the misled Allworthy. The second of these possible verdicts on Tom's case—the one more in keeping with the spirit of the book—would take the tolerant view that Tom's energy, though misdirected throughout much of the novel, nevertheless, reveals an essential warmth of heart absolutely opposed to Blifil's cold "virtue." By looking at the complexities of Tom's case, at his youth and confusion coupled with the apparent hopelessness of his ever finding happiness with Sophia, the more tolerant reader would posit lack of caution or imprudence, perhaps even stupidity, but not innate viciousness.

Complicating the issue, the narrator develops his discussion on the conservation of character by criticizing the practice of comic playwrights:

> Our modern Authors of Comedy have fallen almost
> universally into the Error here hinted at: Their
> Heroes generally are notorious Rogues, and their
> Heroines abandoned Jades, during the first four Acts;

but in the fifth, the former become very worthy
Gentlemen, and the latter, Women of Virtue and
Discretion: Nor is the Writer often so kind as to
give himself the least Trouble, to reconcile or account
for this monstrous Change and Incongruity. There is,
indeed, no other Reason to be assigned for it, than
because the Play is drawing to a Conclusion; as if it
was no less natural in a Rogue to repent in the last
Act of a Play, than in the last of his Life; which we
perceive to be generally the Case at *Tyburn*, a Place
which might, indeed, close the Scene of some Comedies with much Propriety, as the Heroes in these are
most commonly eminent for those very Talents which
not only bring Men to the Gallows, but enable them
to make a heroic Figure when they are there.

(1: 406)

This description of so many Jonathan Wilds, however, is precisely the
sentence that innumerable critics like Johnson have passed on Tom and
Sophia, as well as on the comic reversals that allow for the happy ending.

Although it can be argued that the narrator is here speaking of drama
and not of a comical, epical kind of writing, such a rigid application of genre
would not conclusively settle the case. The narrator obliquely refers to Tom's
own comic reversal, and the references to Tyburn Hill and hanging drive this
particular peg home. These references look back to the introduction of the
adolescent Tom as a lad "born to be hanged" in the introductory essay to
the third book (1: 118). Certainly, these same references to capital
punishment look forward to the narrator's later burlesque complaint in book
17, chapter 1, where he states that Tom's situation has become so critical
that he does not know if he will be able to save him from the gallows by the
"natural" means he has promised to employ (2: 875).

The initial essay to the eighth book, therefore, seems to be designed
not to justify or obscure the marvelous complexities of the comic plot of *Tom
Jones* but rather to bring them to the fore as a defamiliarization of the
plotting of conventional comedies and romances. Ironically, the process also

lays bare and playfully mocks the comic plot of *Tom Jones* itself. Placed immediately after the incident in which the sentry mistakes the wounded Tom for a ghost come to haunt Northerton, this initial essay both plays off the mock apparition and introduces the series of coincidences that take place during Tom and Sophia's travels to London. Not only is this essay followed in the body of book 8 by Tom's meeting with his alleged father, Partridge, but that meeting immediately precedes the Man of the Hill episode and Tom's rescue of Mrs. Waters from her murderous lover, Northerton. Of course, the said Mrs. Waters is Jenny Jones, Tom's alleged mother. Although the narrator states elsewhere that the introductory chapters are interchangeable (2: 832), such placement reveals an artful and ironic intention that exposes the workings of the plot of *Tom Jones*—a comic intention designed to reveal the improbable nature of the series of events that allow Tom to redeem himself in the eyes of Allworthy, Sophia, and tolerant readers.

Given such complex irony and comic convolution, any reading of the introductory chapter to the eighth book as a straightforward, though perhaps witty, Aristotelian argument for a realistic application of probability can only work through a highly selective method. The essay must first be wrenched from its context within the complex textual nexus and then read as a self-standing whole devoid of reference to the work of which it is a part. The critic must next assume that the phrase "a Genius of the highest Rank," which is surely ambiguous, alludes to Pope and not to Martinus Scriblerus so that the quotation from the *Peri Bathous* on the nature of poetic art may be taken as having straightforward consequences to Fielding's theory of fiction. Such a critic has to ignore the narrator's own tendency toward a pedantic show of learning and skill. Finally, a critic wishing to accept the preface to book 8 as a significant argument of Aristotelian principles untarnished by a corrosive irony must refuse to acknowledge the multi-leveled reference back and forth between this chapter and other important segments of the text. To acknowledge such a system of reference is to acknowledge that the essay forces the reader to see the conventional movement of the comic plot toward a happy resolution as replete with improbabilities and, in a final word, as highly and self-consciously artificial.

Notes

1. Ian Watt, *The Rise of the Novel: Studies in Defoe, Richardson, and Fielding* (Berkeley: U of California P, 1957) 288. For a treatment of the novel as other than "formal realism," see Mikhail Bakhtin, "Epic and Novel," *The Dialogic Imagination: Four Essays by M. M. Bakhtin*, trans. Caryl Emerson and Michael Holquist, ed. Michael Holquist (Austin: U of Texas P, 1981) 3–40.

2. Watt 288.

3. Watt 288.

4. Francis Macdonald Cornford, *The Origin of Attic Comedy* (Gloucester: Peter Smith, 1968) 4. Cornford describes the *Parabasis* as such an interruption:
> Of all the strange characteristics of a play by Aristophanes, the one which most forcibly strikes the modern reader is the *Parabasis* of the Chorus—a long passage which cuts the play in two about half way through its course and completely suspends the action. This passage is wholly undramatic. It is delivered by the Chorus and its Leaders, and it normally opens with a farewell to the actors, who leave the stage clear till it is over, and then return to carry on the business of the piece to the end.

5. R. S. Crane, "The Plot of *Tom Jones*," *Journal of General Education* 4 (1950): 127.

6. Francis Coventry, the author of *Pompey the Little* and an admirer of Fielding's work, tells of a humorous comment once made in relation to Fielding's "low" characters:
> I once heard a very fine lady, condemning some highly finished conversations in one of your works, sir, for this curious reason—'because,' she said, 'tis such sort of stuff as passes every day between me and my own maid.'

See Francis Coventry, Dedication, *The History of Pompey the Little or The Life and Adventures of a Lap-dog*, ed. Robert Adams Day (London: Oxford UP, 1974) xliii. For a discussion of Coventry, see Frederic T. Blanchard, *Fielding the Novelist: A Study in Historical Criticism* (New Haven: Yale UP, 1926) 55–57.

7. See John Preston, *The Created Self: The Reader's Role in Eighteenth-Century Fiction* (London: Heinemann, 1970) 114. Preston argues that the effects of reading *Tom Jones* are epistemological, not moral:
> The plot of *Tom Jones*, then, may be best understood in terms of the way it is read. Its structure is the structure of successive responses to the novel. It exists in the reader's attention rather than in the written sequences. This means that its effect is epistemological rather than moral. It helps us to see

how we acquire our knowledge of human experience; it is a clarification of the process of understanding.
Preston's distinction between moral and epistemological, though useful, obscures the fact that Fielding's text forces readers to expose their rigid responses in both moral and intellectual ways. See Wolfgang Iser, *The Implied Reader: Patterns of Communication in Prose Fiction from Bunyan to Becket* (Baltimore: Johns Hopkins UP, 1974) 46–47.

8. Sir Walter Scott, *Sir Walter Scott: On Novelists and Fiction*, ed. Iaon Williams (New York: Barnes & Noble, 1968) 46.

9. Scott 52.

10. Scott 52.

11. Blanchard xi–xii.

12. Wilbur L. Cross, *The History of Henry Fielding*, vol. 2 (1918; New York: Russell & Russell, 1963) 158–76 and F. Homes Dudden, *Henry Fielding: His Life, Work, and Times*, vol. 2 (Hamden: Archon, 1966) 645–51.

13. Cross 2: 176.

14. Dudden 2: 627.

15. Dudden 2: 628.

16. Cross 2: 159–60.

17. Cross 2: 160.

18. Cross 2: 160.

19. Cross 2: 162.

20. Cross 2: 165–66.

21. Watt argues that the apparent contradiction between Johnson's neoclassical theory and his criticism of Fielding marks an example of Johnson's literary insight and that
> the radical honesty of his literary insight raised fundamental issues so forcibly that later criticism cannot but use his formulations as points of departure; any comparison between the two first masters of the novel form certainly must begin from the basis which he provided. (262)

22. Samuel Richardson, *Selected Letters of Samuel Richardson*, ed. John Carroll (Oxford: Clarendon, 1964) 198–99.

23. Fielding has his narrator anticipate this charge of "lowness." In the introductory chapter of book 11, "*A Crust for the Critics*," the narrator treats such critics harshly:

> Such may likewise be suspected of deserving this Character [Slanderer], who without assigning any particular Faults, condemn the whole in general defamatory Terms; such as vile, dull, da—d Stuff, &c. and particularly by the Use of the Monosyllable Low; a Word which becomes the Mouth of no Critic who is not RIGHT HONOURABLE. (2: 570)

24. Richardson 330.

25. Blanchard 145.

26. Aristotle, *De Poetica*, trans. Ingram Bywater, vol. 11 of *The Works of Aristotle*, ed. W. D. Ross (Oxford: Clarendon, 1959) 1448a.

27. James Boswell, *Boswell's Life of Johnson* (London: Oxford UP, 1953) 389.

28. Boswell 389.

29. Boswell 389.

30. Boswell 389. Boswell gives Johnson's view and then offers his own refusal to be convinced. Consequently, although Boswell reports that Johnson would quote Richardson's statement that "the virtues of Fielding's heroes were the vices of a truly good man," he offers his own positive reading of Fielding: "But I cannot help being of the opinion, that the neat watches of Fielding are as well constructed as the large clocks of Richardson, and that his dial-plates are brighter" (389). What is curious here is that Boswell has dismantled Johnson's metaphor by shifting the tenor from the authors' respective knowledge of the heart to the text themselves. The question becomes one of elegance of construction rather than the matter used in the composition.

31. John Dennis, Epistle Dedicatory, *The Advancement and Reformation of Modern Poetry*, vol. 1 of *The Critical Works of John Dennis*, ed. Edward Niles Hooker (Baltimore: Johns Hopkins P, 1939) 202. See also M. H. Abrams, *The Mirror and the Lamp: Romantic Theory and the Critical Tradition* (London: Oxford UP, 1953) 17.

32. Boswell 480. It should be noted that Johnson did read *Amelia* "through without stopping" and that Mrs. Piozzi said Johnson once claimed that Amelia was "the most pleasing heroine of all the romances." See Ronald Paulson and Thomas Lockwood, *Henry Fielding: The Critical Heritage* (London: Routledge and Kegan Paul, 1969) 439, 445.

33. Paulson and Lockwood 443.

34. Samuel Johnson, No. 4, *The Rambler*, ed. W. J. Bate and Albrecht B. Strauss, vol. 3 of *The Yale Edition of the Works of Samuel Johnson* (New Haven: Yale UP, 1969) 19.

35. Johnson, *Rambler* 21.

36. Johnson, *Rambler* 23.

37. Johnson, *Rambler* 24.

38. Samuel Johnson, Preface to the Dictionary, *Johnson's Dictionary: A Modern Selection*, ed. E. L. McAdam, Jr., and George Milne (New York: Pantheon, 1963) 24.

39. Samuel Johnson, Preface to the Dictionary 24.

40. Johnson's criticism of Shakespeare's use of puns implies the same structure as this Newtonian allusion to refraction. Puns, by meaning at least two different and often contradictory things at once, undermine the possibilities of exact and absolute signification. See Samuel Johnson, Preface to Shakespeare, 1756, *Johnson on Shakespeare*, ed. Arthur Sherbo, vol. 7 of *The Yale Edition of the Works of Samuel Johnson* (New Haven: Yale UP, 1968) 74.

41. Johnson, *Rambler* 24. For Auerbach's definition of *figural*, see Erich Auerbach, *Mimesis: The Representation of Reality in Western Literature*, trans. Willard R. Trask (Princeton: Princeton UP, 1953) 555.

42. In chapter 48 of *Rasselas*, the companions visit the Egyptian "catacombs," and, while surrounded by the corruption of generations, they discuss the immortality of the soul. Rasselas remarks that such "missions of the dead" would be melancholy to "him who did not know that he shall never die" (122). The princess shortly follows: "To me, said the princess, the choice of life is become less important; I hope hereafter to think only on the choice of eternity" (122). Such remarks clearly follow the same pattern as Johnson's remarks on the new fiction. The "choice of eternity" subsumes the "choice of life." See Samuel Johnson, *The History of Rasselas, Prince of Abissinia*, ed. J. P. Hardy (1968; Oxford: Oxford UP, 1990) 118–122. For a theoretical discussion of time and setting, see M. M. Bakhtin, "Forms of Time and of the Chronotope in the Novel," *The Dialogic Imagination: Four Essays by M. M. Bakhtin*, trans. Caryl Emerson and Michael Holquist, ed. Michael Holquist (Austin: U of Texas P, 1981) 84–258.

43. Abrams 12–13.

44. Abrams 14.

45. See Michael Irwin, *Henry Fielding: The Tentative Realist* (Oxford: Clarendon, 1967) 2–3. Irwin argues that

> Fielding did have theoretical ideas about the requirements of prose narrative, of course, but his primary concern was always didactic. His choice of techniques within the novels was usually dictated by the cast of his moral views. Some of them could be represented only in terms of action, others only in

terms of character. Some of them demanded a formal embodiment, some a realistic. The form Fielding developed involved an uneasy compromise between these various pressures, and can be adequately studied only with reference to them.

But Irwin's claim of the "uneasy compromise" of Fielding's methods does not account for the possibility that the tension between parts is both methodological and intentional.

46. Quoted from Blanchard 227. For Blanchard's original source, see James Burnett, Lord Monboddo, *Of the Origin and Progress of Language*, vol. 3 (Edinburgh, 1776) 296–98.

47. Quoted from Blanchard 227. For original source, see Monboddo 296–98.

48. Watt 30.

49. Aristotle, *De Poetica* 1448b.

50. See Robert Alter, *Fielding and the Nature of the Novel* (Cambridge: Harvard UP, 1968) 53.

51. Henry Fielding, *Joseph Andrews*, ed. Martin C. Battestin, *The Wesleyan Edition of the Works of Henry Fielding*, ex. ed. W. B. Coley (Middletown: Wesleyan UP, 1967) 162–70.

52. Henry Fielding, *Joseph Andrews* 167.

53. Robert Alter, *Fielding* 56.

54. Robert Alter, *Fielding* 57.

55. Martin C. Battestin and Ruthe R. Battestin, *Henry Fielding: A Life* (London: Routledge, 1989) 314–15. Battestin correctly identifies "the twin essential bases of his [Fielding's] art" when writing of Fielding's letter of September 17, 1741, to James Harris:

This letter is one of the important personal documents of Fielding's life—important in what it reveals of his reading and his mind, of his profound and subtle understanding of what are the twin essential bases of his art: the origins of laughter and the contradictions of human nature.

56. For a discussion of the tensions created in the reader, see Iser, *Implied Reader* 29–56. Mark Kinkead-Weekes makes similar comments:

The big difference moreover, between authorial commentary and authorial irony on the one hand, and the kind of double irony in which both apparent ways of reading are unsatisfactory, is that the latter throws the reader on his own resources and forces him to question his own response, as well as the comic texture out of which the questions arise. And that response cannot be merely a matter of concepts, even moral ones. It must also be a matter of the reader's comic imagination and sense of fun, as well as the writer's.

Mark Kinkead-Weeks, "Out of the Thicket in *Tom Jones*," *Henry Fielding: Justice Observed*, ed. K. G. Simpson (London: Vision, 1985) 141–42.

57. For discussions of the time scheme, see Cross 2: 158–76 and Dudden 2: 645–51.

58. Auerbach 554. For a treatment of Fielding's use of different voices and levels of style, see Henry Knight Miller, "The Voices of Henry Fielding: Style in *Tom Jones*," *The Augustan Milieu: Essays Presented to Louis A. Landa*, ed. Henry Knight Miller, Eric Rothstein, and G. S. Rousseau (Oxford: Clarendon, 1970) 262–88.

59. Auerbach 554–55.

60. Ford Madox Ford, *Critical Writings of Ford Madox Ford*, ed. Frank MacShane, Regents Critics Series, gen. ed. Paul A. Olson (Lincoln: U of Nebraska P, 1964) 10–11.

61. See Michael Irwin 98. Irwin complains that "various practices combine to prevent *Tom Jones* from becoming in fact what in theory it could have been: a novel whose moral significance was expressed wholly through its characters and the complex plot in which they are involved."

62. Watt 252.

63. Watt 252–53.

64. Alexander Pope, *Peri Bathous: or, Martinus Scriblerus, His Treatise of the Art of Sinking in Poetry*, ed. Rosemary Cowler, vol. 2 of *The Prose Works of Alexander Pope* (Hamden: Archon, 1986) 192.

65. Watt 253.

66. Preston observes that Shaftesbury attacks "modern" authors who put themselves forward in their works in his "Advice to an Author" (115–16). This "modern" trait, of course, is exactly what Fielding's narrator exhibits continually.

67. Aristotle, *De Poetica* 1451b.

68. Henry Fielding, *The Journal of a Voyage to Lisbon, by the Late Henry Fielding, Esq.*, ed. Austin Dobson, vol. 16 of *The Complete Works of Henry Fielding, Esq.*, ed. William Ernest Henley (1903; New York: Barnes & Noble, 1967) 181–82.

69. Henry Fielding, *The Covent-Garden Journal*, ed. Gerard Edward Jensen, vol. 1 (New York: Russell & Russell, 1964) 205–12.

CHAPTER
3

The Selective Voice and Necessary Deception

*These writers systematically disrupt the distinctions their readers
require in order fully to understand, even though they claim that
the distinctions are vitally important.*

Dennis A. Foster

Fielding's disruptive narrator in *Tom Jones* emphasizes the *told* quality of the
text, emphasizes, that is, the *telling*, the actual activity of narration. His
characteristic intrusions force the reader toward an awareness of his presence,
dispelling, as a consequence, the illusion of a clear, unmediated presentation
of things as they are. The visibility of such a narrative presence is enhanced
by the narrator's continual references to the acts of reading and writing, as
well as by his discussions of the processes of interpretation and critical evaluation offered throughout the text. The narrator's introductory essays, his
many intrusions, possible interpretations of circumstances, and predictions of
consequences all function in the text to create a convoluted play of comic
devices—a play that makes the existence of the various devices of narration
visible in a way that lays bare the constructive selectivity of a narrative voice
that reveals itself through the act of narration.

Any narration, any writing, or, for that matter, any use of language, will
of necessity be determined by some theory of selection, some principle of
inclusion and exclusion. Nonetheless, the usual process of everyday usage
obscures the structural paradigms that control any commonplace utterance.
In its everyday aspect, language is transparent, and naïve realism, in its
attempt to mirror the everyday, attempts as well to remain a transparent

medium of reference to the thing itself. The message dominates the medium, or, as Ian Watt argues, "the function of language is much more largely referential in the novel than in other literary forms."[1] But such a claim is only valid for the realistic novel, the "formal realism," that is, that Watt contends constitutes the defining characteristic of the genre.

Watt's claim that "the genre itself works by exhaustive presentation rather than by elegant concentration," although descriptive of Richardson's methods, unfairly weighs the scales against Fielding's.[2] It is true that in his preface to *Joseph Andrews* Fielding asserts that the "comic Romance" or "comic Epic-Poem in Prose" differs from comic drama "as the serious Epic from Tragedy: its Action being more extended and comprehensive; containing a much larger Circle of Incidents, and introducing a greater Variety of Characters."[3] *Tom Jones* itself is, indeed, a long narrative that contains a large cast of characters and covers a great expanse of Georgian England. Still, Fielding's narrator in *Tom Jones* explicitly counters the movement toward purely referential language and "exhaustive presentation" by his theory of narrative selection which, in its own way, argues for the "elegant concentration" that Ian Watt denies to the novel as a genre.

In the introductory chapter to the second book of *Tom Jones*, the narrator maintains that a "History," in contrast to a "News-Paper," should only concentrate on those periods during which important events have happened. Entitling this chapter *"Shewing what Kind of a History this is; what it is like, and what it is not like,"* the narrator here proclaims his "new Province of Writing" and declares that, as the founder, he may dictate the relevant laws himself, although he does soften his claims by maintaining that his administration is solely directed toward the reader's ease and comfort (1: 77–78). Proposing that his "History" will "pursue the Method of those Writers who profess to disclose the Revolutions of Countries" rather than those who merely record the flow of events and "keep even Pace with Time" (1: 75–76), the narrator achieves two distinct effects.

On the one hand, he lends a heightened significance to his "History" by linking it to the historical events in the rise and fall of nations. He broadens, as it were, the local significance of the story of Tom and Sophia.

This gain in significance is specifically reinforced by the narrator's use of the Forty-five, for, throughout the middle section of the text in books 7 through 12, the narrator links Tom's travels to the invasion of England by Bonnie Prince Charles and, consequently, to the Jacobite threat to the Protestant Britain.   Also, Squire Western's own Jacobitism, his drinking to the king across the water, as well as the Jacobitism of Partridge, Tom's traveling companion and alleged father, all add to the web that ties Tom's travels to the momentous events of the winter of 1745.   Not only does Tom himself march with the King's troopers toward the north as a volunteer for a brief time, but, during her own travels, Sophia is ironically mistaken for Jenny Cameron, the alleged bonnie lass of Bonnie Prince Charles, by a Jacobite landlord (2: 591−94).[4]

On the other hand, beyond heightening the significance of his central characters by linking them to such events of national importance, the narrator also foregrounds his own reflexive methods and denigrates those of Richardson.   In contrast to the "voluminous Historian" whose histories are like a "Stage-Coach, which performs constantly the same Course, empty as well as full" (1: 75−76), the narrator maintains that he will pass over those times during which nothing of import happened (1: 76).   In the case of "any extraordinary Scene," however, he insists that he will "spare no Pains nor Paper to open it at large to our Reader" (1: 76).   Using the editorial *we*, the narrator states that

> if whole Years should pass without producing any
> thing worthy his [the reader's] Notice, we shall not be
> afraid of a Chasm in our History; but shall hasten on
> to Matters of Consequence, and leave such Periods
> of Time totally unobserved. (1: 76)

What is given to the reader will, in other words, be filtered through the narrator.   Applying his principle of selection, he will determine what is and what is not of "Consequence" in the construction of his tale.

Following this statement of principle, the narrator warns his readers, asserting that they should not be surprised by any gaps in coverage or sudden leaps forward to such events as those he considers to be of importance to his narrative:

> My Reader then is not to be surprised, if in the Course of this Work, he shall find some Chapters very short, and others altogether as long; some that contain only the Time of a single Day, and others that comprise Years; in a word, if my History sometimes seems to stand still, and sometimes to fly. For all which I shall not look on myself as accountable to any Court of Critical Jurisdiction whatever: For as I am, in reality, the Founder of a new Province of Writing, so I am at liberty to make what Laws I please therein.... (1: 77)

Although such selection is necessary to any literary composition, the temporal play that the narrator announces here as his constitutional right foregrounds the act of interpretation that he must make to construct his plot. He must decide which events are those of "Consequence" and which are not. The narrator must, in short, pick and choose, include and exclude, and his insistence on this very point functions to make his plotting of Tom's story visible to his readers.

The narrator, indeed, calls attention to his principle of selection throughout *Tom Jones*. Not only in his introductory chapters but also in the humorous titles to the various books, the narrator emphasizes his process of selecting only those periods that he deems of importance. The first book, entitled "*Containing as much of the Birth of the Foundling as is necessary or proper to acquaint the Reader with in the Beginning of this History*," immediately informs the reader that selections have been made according to the narrator's plan and judgment. He has sifted events. His ideas of necessity and propriety will determine what readers will learn about the circumstances surrounding Tom's birth and when they will learn it.

After this initial introduction to the narrator's assertion of choice, all of the following books contain some indication of the length of time covered, and books 3 through 10 give increasingly extensive treatment to increasingly shorter periods of time. The second book, "*Containing Scenes of matrimonial Felicity in different Degrees of Life; and various other Transactions during the first two Years after the Marriage between Captain* Blifil, *and Miss* Bridget Allworthy," concentrates on the marriage of Tom's natural mother and that of his nominal father, Partridge, covering, as the title of the book indicates, roughly two years. Book 3 marks a jump forward of twelve years, and its title announces that it will cover "*the Time when* Tommy Jones *arrived at the Age of Fourteen, till he attained the Age of Nineteen.*"

After the third book, however, the time periods covered by each of the following books are radically shortened. Book 4 contains "*the Time of a Year.*" The fifth book covers "*a Portion of Time, somewhat longer than Half a Year.*" Book 6 contains the events of "*about three Weeks*," and book 7 deals with a mere "*three Days.*" In its turn, the eighth book, "*Containing above two Days*," reduces the time covered by approximately twenty-four hours. The following two, books 9 and 10, both cover approximately twelve hours. These two books, of course, deal with the highly concentrated jumble of events at the famous inn at Upton and those immediately following.

The next eight books cover the events of some thirty-six days, but the neat pattern of increasingly extensive treatment of shortening periods of time is not strictly followed. Books 11 and 12 both deal with the events of "*about three Days*," yet those in the thirteenth cover twelve days. Combined, books 14 and 15 cover four more days, but 16 and 17 increase the time to three days apiece. Of the last book, the eighteenth one, the title indicates that the time contained is "*about Six Days*," but the last chapter, "*In which the History is concluded*," broadens this period into the short sketches of the happily married life of Tom and Sophia, as well as the meting out of the various poetically justified sentences to Allworthy, Western, Blifil, and the other characters of note, covering the events of early 1746 on into the timelessness of the comic ending.

The significant point is that in seventeen of the eighteen books in *Tom Jones* the narrator emphasizes the period of time covered in that particular book, thereby, illustrating his claims in the introductory essay to the second book that he will ignore periods during which nothing of "Consequence" to his narrative happened but will, nevertheless, expend the necessary effort and considerable paper during his narration of those events of importance that he does offer for the reader's perusal. This emphasis given to the narrator's selectiveness foregrounds his claims, but, at the same time, it also makes the process of narrative selection itself visible to the reader. Unlike Richardson's or Defoe's circumstantial methods, Fielding's reflexive narrator calls attention to himself and the actual operation of his narration. Such insistence continually asserts that the text is not an unmediated copy of reality; rather, it is product of rhetoric, a human construction actively organized by a selective human intelligence.

In the introductory essay to book 3, ironically entitled *"Containing little or nothing,"* the narrator continues the process of actively discussing his theory of narrative selection. After reminding the reader of his assertions in the introductory chapter on his selectiveness from the second book, the narrator maintains that his method promotes the reader's comfort and aids in the free play of the intellect:

> In so doing, we do not only consult our own Dignity and Ease; but the Good and Advantage of the Reader: For besides, that by these Means we prevent him from throwing away his Time in reading either without Pleasure or Emolument, we give him at all such Seasons an Opportunity of employing that wonderful Sagacity, of which he is Master, by filling up these vacant Spaces of Time with his own Conjectures; for which Purpose, we have taken care to qualify him in the preceding Pages. (1: 116)

Here, the narrator ironically plays on the *"little or nothing"* indicated in the title of the essay by juxtaposing the reader's pleasure and enlightenment. Although he contends that it would be a mere waste of time to read about the inconsequential events that he sees fit to exclude from his narrative, he still offers the space, as it were, for the reader to write, to employ a "wonderful Sagacity" in interpretative finesse. Not only does this ironic call for thought force the reader consciously to take the actions depicted in the text as something of more substance than mere romancing, but it also playfully denigrates the reader's ability.

The narrator immediately follows this ironic passage with two examples of the kind of interpretative activity to which he is alluding. Illustrating his case, he offers a paragraph on Mr. Allworthy and one on his sister, Bridget, and their respective reaction to the death of Bridget's husband, Captain Blifil. As is usual with this narrator, these two sketches are diametrically opposed. The narrator's reflections on Mr. Allworthy deal with internal substance and intellectual activity. They reflect the manner in which such a man as Allworthy would use philosophy and religion to overcome the grief he would feel at the loss of his brother-in-law (1: 116−17). The passage on Bridget, however, deals only in surface effects, only in the fashion of grief and not in the commonplace but nevertheless substantial reflections of the stoical use of the intellectual to moderate worldly loss. Bridget, in short, "conducted herself through the whole Season in which Grief is to make its Appearance on the Outside of the Body, with the strictest Regard to all the Rules of Custom and Decency" (1: 117).

This contrast between stoic philosophy and fashionable widowhood subtly implies the narrator's disingenuousness. Although his plot demands that he emphasize the flawed goodness of Mr. Allworthy in his upcoming condemnation of Tom, the plot also requires that the character of Bridget be obscured since the entire plot hinges on maintaining the secret of Tom's birth until the proper time and place. Consequently, in the paragraph offering Mr. Allworthy's reaction to the death of his brother-in-law, the narrator speaks of "those Emotions of Grief, which on such Occasions enter into all Men whose Hearts are not composed of Flint, or their Heads of as solid Materials" (1: 116). Through the consistent practice of "Philosophy and Religion," a person might sustain the loss without undue grief or lamentation, for they "enable a strong and religious Mind to take leave of a Friend on his Deathbed with little less Indifference than if he was preparing for a long Journey" (1: 116−17).

The following paragraph dealing with Bridget, however, implies the lack of internal substance by treating only the external manifestations of fashionable grief. The narrator insists that the "Appearance on the Outside of the Body" follows the decorum of widowhood with "the strictest Regard to all the Rules of Custom and Decency" (1: 117). As the widow's weeds graduate from the deepest black toward white, "so did her [Bridget's] Countenance change from Dismal to Sorrowful, from Sorrowful to Sad, and from Sad to Serious, till the Day came in which she was allowed to return to her former Serenity" (1: 117). Indeed, the whole implication of the contrast here between brother and sister is one of worth and integrity of character. The brother is worthy and sound, but the sister is shallow, addicted to custom, to, that is, the mere forms, the symbols, rather than the substance. Ironically, such a narrative move directs the reader away from any serious consideration of Bridget as Tom's true natural mother. She appears to be merely a conventional hypocrite, a stickler for the social forms, a totally inappropriate source for the warm-natured Tom. Furthermore, the narrator's description of these two siblings' reactions to the death of a member of their family supports the deception of Jenny Jones's false confession to Allworthy that she was Tom's mother, a deception necessary if the narrator is to complete his birth-mystery plot.

Immediately following his contrasting examples of interpretative finesse, the narrator returns to his mocking play on his reader's abilities in the art of criticism. He first acknowledges two distinct classes of readers and then extends his irony:

> We have mentioned these two as Examples only of the Task which may be imposed on Readers of the lowest Class. Much higher and harder Exercises of Judgment and Penetration may reasonably be expected from the upper Graduates in Criticism. Many notable Discoveries will, I doubt not, be made by such, of the Transactions which happened in the Family of our worthy Man, during all the Years which we have thought proper to pass over: For tho'

> nothing worthy of a Place in this History occurred
> within that Period; yet did several Incidents happen,
> of equal Importance with those reported by the daily
> and weekly Historians of the Age, in reading which,
> great Numbers of Persons consume a considerable
> Part of their Time, very little, I am afraid, to their
> Emolument. (1: 117)

These claims both reinforce the narrator's theory of selection and, at the same time, openly challenge readers, for the sneer involved in the distinction between lower and upper class readers implies that any undue critical activity will involve a foolish waste of their limited time and energy. Such unproductive activity on the part of readers will be wasteful, the narrator implies, because it concentrates on matters extraneous to his conception of the history that he is narrating. In fact, the narrator's snub of "the upper Graduates in Criticism" further indicates that he believes undue critical delving into the periods that he considers to be blank merely reveals the intellectual vanity of readers assured of their own insight.

This rhetorical device also supports the narrator's necessary deception involved in the development of the plot in a manner similar to his contrasting paragraphs on Allworthy and Bridget. Although the narrator insists that he has the welfare of his readers in mind whenever he applies his principles of selection, he also maintains his awareness of the reader's "wonderful Sagacity." "As we are sensible," the narrator writes, "that much the greatest Part of our Readers are very eminently possessed of this Quality, we have left them a Space of twelve Years to exert it in..." (1: 118). The irony here is lodged in the contradictory directions of the two different assertions. On the one hand, the narrator claims that his selectiveness is necessary for the reader's good, but, on the other, he allows the blank and irrelevant periods for the "good" of the reader's creative "Sagacity." The irony, in fact, forestalls the offer, leaving readers with the choice of either accepting the narrator's judgment on the "consequence" of events or admitting that they, like those "upper Graduates in Criticism," expand their limited resources in the pursuit of the irrelevant.[5]

Indeed, the heightened language of the narrator's offer also functions to undermine the offer itself. Phrases, such as "employing that wonderful Sagacity," "higher and harder Exercises of Judgment and Penetration," "upper Graduates in Criticism," and "eminently possessed of this Quality," all work to indicate a contempt that the narrator directs toward those readers who hold their interpretative abilities in high esteem. No doubt, this challenge looks forward to the introductory chapters of book 10, "*Containing Instruction very necessary to be perused by modern Critics*," and book 11, "*A Crust for the Critics*," in which the narrator confronts the problem of critics and criticism directly. Nonetheless, in the first chapter of book 3, the narrator both maintains his theory of selection and intimidates readers while offering interpretative paradigms that in fact reinforce the deception he must maintain to construct the elaborate plot of *Tom Jones*. He reveals his narrative presence by continual intrusions, claiming a trustworthiness because of his openness that his actual performance belies, for, while the narrator asserts his principle of selection, he also carefully directs his readers away from any serious inquiry into those areas that he must disguise if he is to complete his plot with the revelation of the facts surrounding the birth and discovery of the infant Tom.

The narrator's consistent practice of narrative deception in *Tom Jones* is once again illustrated by the metaphorical embellishment that he gives to his selective methods in the introductory chapter to book 2. Recalling with this new figure the sophistic implications of his insistence in the "Bill of Fare" from the first chapter of book 1, that the difference between a good book and a bad one, between one book found to be "natural" and another declared "unnatural," resides in the author's "Cookery," the narrator compares his own selective methodology to the *modus operandi* employed by the operatives of the state lottery:

> These [times] are indeed to be considered as Blanks
> in the grand Lottery of Time. We therefore who are
> the Registers of that Lottery, shall imitate those
> sagacious Persons who deal in that which is drawn at

Guild-Hall, and who never trouble the Public with the
many Blanks they dispose of; but when a great Prize
happens to be drawn, the News-Papers are presently
filled with it, and the World is sure to be informed at
whose Office it was sold: Indeed, commonly two or
three different Offices lay claim to the Honour of
having disposed of it; by which I suppose the Adventurers are given to understand that certain Brokers
are in the Secrets of Fortune, and indeed of her
Cabinet-Council. (1: 76–77)

The state lottery, which operated from 1694 to 1826, was often a target for
Fielding's satire.[6] But in this passage, the narrator identifies himself with the
"Registers of that Lottery," and, consequently, he connects himself and his
own method of narrative selection to the deception that he indicates was
practiced on the public by the announcement of the winners but not the
odds in the drawing. For, since neither the registers nor the brokers ever
"trouble the Public with the many Blanks they dispose of," then the publication of the winners would, in fact, present a distorted picture of the odds
given on instant wealth.

Nonetheless, the narrator ironically reveals his own pretensions toward
a special insight into the operations of Fortune. Although apparently attempting to distinguish his own narrative selection from the unselective
broadcast of the "New-Papers," the narrator actually implicates his own
selection when he criticizes the publishers of newspapers for deceiving "the
Adventurers" by the manner in which the brokers who sold (or who claim to
have sold) the winning tickets are presented as being the ministers to
Fortune. The implication that such brokers have some uncommon insight
into the dark operations of Fortune parallels the narrator's claim that he is
capable of making the proper and significant selections from raw events to
produce a meaningful and entertaining narrative that is constructed with
unusual concern for the reader's ease. To be sure, *Tom Jones* is a retrospective narration; still, the narrator does lay claim to special abilities in his
claims of significant selectiveness, and his alleged omniscience is here linked

to at least a faint accusation of duplicity and public deception through these metaphorical implications of the dubious monetary motivation behind the selection and publication of information that echo the opening assertion of what an author ought to be in book 1, chapter 1.

As the narrator claims in the "Bill of Fare" that an author should "consider himself, not as a Gentleman who gives a private or eleemosynary Treat, but rather as one who keeps a public Ordinary, at which all Persons are welcome for their Money" (1: 31), so, in the introductory chapter to the second book, the narrator implies that his narrative selections parallel the duplicity in the general operation of the state lottery. As his interpretative examples in the two paragraphs in chapter 1, book 3, on Mr. Allworthy's and Bridget's individual reactions to the death of Captain Blifil mock the readers, so, in the introductory essay to book 2, the narrator implies by his metaphor that his readers, like "the Adventurers" taken in by the publication of the offices that reportedly sold lucky tickets, are in their own way dupes of the narration and the narrator's selective control. In its turn, this implication parallels the challenge that the narrator makes in his acknowledgment of the classes of his readers and the slur implied in the rhetorical play involved in the description of the activities of those "upper Graduates in Criticism" (1: 117). Apparently offering the reader control, the narrator continually turns the tables, and these various rhetorical moves recall the similar move made in the first introductory chapter where, after maintaining that an author is at the service of his readers, the narrator contends that with his skill in cookery he may, as the emperor Heliogabalus kept guests eating, keep his readers reading forever if only he supply them with the proper spices and distribution of dishes (1: 33–34).

Such a complex movement of reference and counterreference that both alludes to past chapters and prefigures future ones is not the only significant example of the narrator's involvement in narrative duplicity in *Tom Jones*. The narrator actually introduces the issue into his own narrative of both Tom's adventures after his expulsion from Paradise Hall and of Sophia's subsequent travels. After he has been expelled from Paradise Hall and its environs by the mistaken "justice" of Mr. Allworthy, Tom narrates his own story to Little Benjamin, the comical barber-surgeon who is, in fact, Tom's nominal father, Partridge. The narrator quickly disposes of Tom's narration in a brief summary:

> *Jones* now began, and related the whole History, forgetting only a Circumstance or two, namely, every thing which passed on that Day in which he had fought with *Thwackum*, and ended with his Resolution to go to Sea, till the Rebellion in the North had made him change his Purpose, and had brought him to the Place where he then was. (1: 419–20)

Tom's omission of such central events leading to his sudden expulsion from Paradise Hall renders his personal narrative both suspect and misleading, and the narrator immediately follows his summary of Tom's narration with a discussion of just this particular point. The narrator, however, reinforces his point by employing the comical Partridge as his critical spokesman.

First, the narrator briefly describes Partridge's reaction (or, to be more precise, Little Benjamin's since the narrator has not yet made the revelation of his true identity):

> Little *Benjamin*, who had been all Attention, never once interrupted the Narrative; but when it was ended, he could not help observing, that there must be surely something more invented by his Enemies, and told Mr. *Allworth*y against him, or so good a Man would never have dismissed one he had loved so tenderly, in such a manner. To which *Jones* answered, 'He doubted not but such villanous Arts had been made use of to destroy him.' (1: 420)[7]

Although the reader has to construct Tom's possible narration since it is not given verbatim in the text, Partridge's reaction clearly points to its inadequacy as an explanation of the events that led to Tom's expulsion from his foster home. Also, Partridge's insight into the limitations of Tom's narration can be seen as markedly uncharacteristic of this comic figure—as, for that matter, is his silence throughout its duration—when this instance of critical insight is contrasted to Partridge's more characteristic reactions to the Old Man of the Hill's history and to Garrick's performance in *Hamlet* that Tom takes him to see once they arrive in London.[8]

Following this paragraph dealing with Partridge's critical reaction to Tom's narration, the narrator makes a series of general comments first dealing with Tom's particular narrative and then with the characteristics of first-person narration itself. Verifying Partridge's criticism, the narrator offers his own characterization of Tom's effort:

> And surely it was scarce possible for any one to have avoided making the same Remark with the Barber; who had not, indeed, heard from *Jones* one single Circumstance upon which he was condemned; for his Actions were not now placed in those injurious Lights, in which they had been misrepresented to *Allworthy*: Nor could he mention those many false Accusations which had been from time to time preferred against him to *Allworthy*; for with none of these he was himself acquainted. He had likewise, as we have observed, omitted many material Facts in his present Relation. Upon the whole, indeed, every thing now appeared in such favorable Colours to *Jones*, that Malice itself would have found it no easy Matter to fix any Blame upon him. (1: 420)

Beyond merely verifying Partridge's response, however, the narrator actually extends the charges made against Tom's narrative validity. Here the "Circumstance or two" missing from Tom's narrative that the narrator had originally mentioned is enlarged to the omission of many of the pertinent facts. To be sure, Tom did not have a complete knowledge of the extent of the charges laid against him, as the narrator admits, but the narrator still makes it clear that Tom put his proverbial best foot forward when telling his story to Partridge.

This charge against Tom's veracity is immediately followed by a softening that, while relieving Tom of any real moral culpability in his narrative omissions, ironically implicates the act of first-person narration itself in an inherent duplicity:

> Not that *Jones* desired to conceal or to disguise the Truth; nay, he would have been more unwilling to have suffered any Censure to fall on Mr. *Allworthy* for punishing him, than on his own Actions for deserving it; but, in Reality, so it happened, and so it always will happen: For let a Man be never so honest, the Account of his own Conduct will, in Spite of himself, be so very favourable, that his Vices will come purified through his Lips, and, like foul Liquors well strained, will leave all their Foulness behind. For tho' the Facts themselves may appear, yet so different will be the Motives, Circumstances, and Consequences, when a Man tells his own Story, and when his Enemy tells it, that we scarce can recognize the Facts to be one and the same. (1: 420)

Such a description of narrative relativity not only offers a justification for Tom's own application of narrative selectiveness, but it also reflects on the narrator's own motives, on his own self-interestedness, and on his friendliness toward his hero.

On the most immediate level, these passages dealing with Tom's telling of his own story, Partridge's critical response, and the narrator's general reflections upon the limitations of first-person narration all function as devices in the characterization of Tom himself. They, in effect, help to define his naïve good-heartedness. On a higher level of abstraction, the comments on the inherent self-interest of personal narrative also represent a satiric slap at the pseudo-autobiographical methods of Richardson and Defoe. On a still higher level of abstraction, the narrator's criticism of the inevitable relativity of first-person narrative turns upon an inherent weakness in the act of narration itself and, consequently, upon his own narration of *Tom Jones*.

Throughout these passages, three specific charges are leveled against acts of narration: limited knowledge, self-interestedness, and malicious use. The first, limited knowledge, applies specifically to Tom's lack of knowledge of the stories told about him to Mr. Allworthy by his detractors, Thwackum, Square, and Blifil. In other words, Tom cannot formulate a truly effective narrative of self-justification because he does not know (in contrast to the reader, of course) what has been reported about him to his judge. Such a limitation to the veracity and effectiveness of any first-person narration is obviously inherent in its limited perspective, in its limited point of view. Nevertheless, the next two charges leveled against narration by the narrator involve more closely the necessary duplicity of narrative acts—a duplicity whose origin is ironically located in the very selectiveness that the narrator touts in his introductory essays to the second and third books.

The narrator maintains that self-interest will always slant any personal narrative to the advantage of the teller, "let a Man be never so honest." The necessary limitations of perspective will lead a man to put a favorable interpretation on the facts that he relates about himself, even, as it were, "in Spite of himself." No narration can ever be taken as an unmediated report of events, as a merely transparent relation of circumstances, because narrative selectiveness will manifest itself in the construction of motives and consequences through the narrative act. Not only will narrators be limited by their own personal experiences, limited, in short, by what they know, but individual character will also prescribe the interpretative slant of any narration, even when, as with good-hearted Tom, the narrator attempts to be essentially honest and objective.

In addition to the problems of limited perspective, the narrative act can, as the narrator intimates and as Partridge hypothesizes, be employed as a weapon since any series of raw events can be plotted into any number of different and contradictory narrations. The important distinction here is that between *story*, or the raw events, and the *plot*, or the construction of those events into a narrative. E. M. Forster, for example, bases his discussion of the story/plot distinction on the issue of causation in his *Aspects of the Novel*. For him, the story is simply the series of events, the "What would happen next?," and, as such, *story* is "the lowest and simplest of literary organisms."[9] The plot, on the other hand, represents an interpretative act: "We have," Forster writes, "defined a story as a narrative of events in their time-sequence. A plot is also a narrative of events, the emphasis falling on causality."[10] Significantly, it is exactly the human causal factor that the narrator of *Tom Jones* asserts allows narrators to manipulate, either with a malicious intent or in a fundamentally innocent and unconscious manner, when he maintains that "so different will be the Motives, Circumstances, and Consequences, when a Man tells his own Story, and when his Enemy tells it, that we scarce can recognize the Facts to be one and the same" (1: 420).

Such a treatment of narration as inherently duplicitous as this account by the narrator in his relation of Tom's own telling of his personal narrative to Partridge receives reinforcement from the reader's knowledge that the narratives designed by Thwackum, Square, and Blifil have been used to maneuver Allworthy into his expulsion of Tom from Paradise Hall. Also, these same assertions ironically rebound upon the narrator's own practice. Although he narrates the events from a third-person point of view, the questions of limitations, self-interestedness, and intentions all still apply. Furthermore, since the narrator makes himself a character visible to the reader through his intrusions into the narrative with his suggestions of possible readings, his mock forgetfulness, and, of course, his introductory essays, much of his narrative assumes a first-person perspective, making it directly open to the narrator's own critique of the narrative act.

These multiple ironies are further complicated by the fact that the narrator repeatedly treats parallel circumstances throughout *Tom Jones*. In a series of chapters in book 8 that closely follow Tom's narration to Partridge and the subsequent discussion, the narrator allows the misanthropic Old Man of the Hill to tell his own story of self-righteous indignation at man's proverbial inhumanity to man, a narration centered on the paradoxical thesis that, in the old man's words, "great Philanthropy chiefly inclines us to avoid

and detest Mankind" (1: 450).[11] Beyond the proximity of this account to the
narrator's discussion of Tom's own narration, the debate between Tom and
the old man over the merit of his ill-natured conclusions emphasizes the
limitations and self-deception involved in the old man's misanthropic position.

The narrator follows a similar pattern in his treatment of the narrations
of Mrs. Fitzpatrick and Sophia following their meeting on the road after the
complications that occurred at the inn in Upton. Mrs. Fitzpatrick, Sophia's
runaway cousin who had married an Irish fortune hunter from whom she is
now fleeing, narrates her version of her own story, while Sophia takes the
part of a critical audience.[12] Sophia's response to her cousin's tale parallels
Tom's role in relation to the Old Man of the Hill's narrative. The critical
reactions of both Tom and Sophia function as devices that reinforce the
serious limitations and self-interested intentions of the Old Man of the Hill
and Mrs. Fitzpatrick as revealed by their respective narratives, but Tom's
and Sophia's reactions also serve to define their characters through the
presentation of the antithetical other. Yet the significant point here is that
the narrator, while advancing the characterization of his major characters,
still involves both his hero and his heroine in telling their own tales and
reacting to the personal narratives of others. Humanizing Tom and Sophia
by giving the necessary touches of human frailty, this device also allows the
narrator to return continually to the subject of narration and to offer a series
of examples of its limitations.

Consequently, immediately following Mrs. Fitzpatrick's history, the
narrator deals with Sophia's own narrative. As with the earlier example of
Tom's narration, the narrator here offers a short description and then commentary on Sophia's statement of her own case:

> Sophia now, at the Desire of her Cousin, related—
> not what follows, but what hath gone before in this
> History: For which Reason the Reader will, I sup-
> pose, excuse me, for not repeating it over again.
>
> One Remark, however, I cannot forbear making on
> her Narrative, namely, that she made no more men-
> tion of *Jones*, from the Beginning to the End, than if

there had been no such Person alive. This I will
neither endeavour to account for, nor to excuse.
Indeed, if this may be called a Kind of Dishonesty, it
seems the more inexcusable, from the apparent Openness and explicit Sincerity of the other Lady.—But so
it was. (2: 602)

The narrator's ironic characterization of Mrs. Fitzpatrick's narration as open
and sincere signifies the fundamental dishonesty of that lady's version of her
own story. Nevertheless, Sophia's selectiveness further draws the question of
the inherent duplicity of narration and narrative selection into the open for
the reader's consideration. Also, it should be noted that a large measure of
Sophia's anger with Tom results not simply from her discovery of his sexual
involvement with Mrs. Waters at the Upton inn but also from the fact that
she believes Tom has told a narrative about her to any ready audience
throughout the countryside, although, in fact, Partridge rather than Tom is
the culprit. Ultimately, Sophia's distaste for such a violation of her modesty
implicates the narrator's own broadcast of her story in *Tom Jones* itself.

Such continual notice given to the actual act of narration throughout
Tom Jones emphasizes the action of telling a story and its constitutional
weaknesses and implications. Still, *Tom Jones* is not the only text in which
Fielding has constructed a narrative voice that shows, in one way or another,
a concern for the narrative act as a means of both revelation and deception.
The parodic intent of *Shamela* exposes the limitations of Richardson's
epistolary method and its reliance on first-person narration. The ironic
great/good discourse in *Jonathan Wild* brings the question to the forefront,
particularly in Mrs. Heartfree's narration of her own adventures. *Joseph
Andrews*, in its turn, also treats the issue with the two letters that Joseph
writes to his sister, Pamela. Treating Lady Booby's sexual advances, these
letters reveal a rather narrow meanness from which Joseph's character does
not fully recover until the revelation of his love for Fanny Goodwill softens
his propensity for self-righteous gossip.[13]

In spite of Joseph's momentary slip into the epistolary method, perhaps
the most significant parallels to the narrator's treatment of the narrative act

in *Tom Jones* are those that can be gathered from Fielding's prose satire, *Jonathan Wild*. Mrs. Heartfree's narration of her convoluted adventures establishes a tension between her function in the text as a paradigm of wifely virtue and her actions as a narrator—a tension between paradigm and action that, with appropriate variations, is also present in Sophia's modest narrative reserve in *Tom Jones*. As Mrs. Heartfree tells her tale of repetitive danger and sudden escape, she begins to experience the very real power she exercises over her audience in her new character of narrator. Heartfree, her husband who has just been rescued from the gallows, is, of course, an anxious listener who remains, as it were, suspended in his anxiety while his wife spins her tale. At one point near the beginning of Mrs. Heartfree's narration, she interrupts her narrative to question her husband about his reaction to her diction:

> 'The captain of the privateer was so strong that he apprehended no danger but from a man-of-war, which the sailors discerned this not to be. He therefore struck his colors, and furled his sails as much as possible, in order to lie by and expect her, hoping she might be a prize.' (Here Heartfree smiling, his wife stopped and inquired the cause. He told her it was from her using the sea-terms so aptly: she laughed, and answered he would wonder less at this when he heard the long time she had been on board: and then proceeded.)[14]

The parenthetical intrusion here justifies Mrs. Heartfree's use of "sea-terms" on straightforward empirical grounds. During her adventures, she had lived on board ship among sailors and, consequently, had acquired a degree of naval jargon. Nevertheless, the incident also throws emphasis on Mrs. Heartfree's role as narrator. Not only is she attempting with her use of "sea-terms" to create an effective and colorful narrative of her adventures, but she also turns her husband's somewhat condescending smile back upon him by using the incident with rhetorical purpose. When Mrs. Heartfree asserts that her husband would wonder less—would, in other words, have less reason to smile—once he had heard of all her experiences, she actually heightens her husband's suspense, leading him to painful expectations of as yet untold dangers and domestic calamities.

Elsewhere during her narrative, Mrs. Heartfree once again reveals the delight she personally takes in the power that her role as a narrator gives her over her audience. While telling of one of the numerous attempts made on her virtue during her travels, she exploits suspense for narrative effect in a manner that causes real distress to her husband:

> 'I now passed several days pretty free from the captain's molestation, till one fatal night.' Here, perceiving Heartfree grew pale, she comforted him by an assurance that Heaven had preserved her chastity, and again had restored her unsullied to his arms. She continued thus: 'Perhaps I gave it a wrong epithet in the word fatal; but a wretched night I am sure I may call it, for no woman who came off victorious was, I believe, ever in greater danger.'[15]

The ironic tension in this passage is created by the conflict between Mrs. Heartfree's function in *Jonathan Wild* as both the paradigmatic wife and as a narrator striving to tell an effective tale. Rather than immediately assuring her husband, she launches into her long narrative that, following romance conventions, is replete with "fatal nights" and all of the other paraphernalia of distressed virtue. Ironically, the ideal wife would have slighted her numerous trials and dangers encountered with a simple summary emphasizing her safe return. But to tell an effective narrative, a narrator is obligated to expand, to create suspense and then to maintain the tension. Successful narration dwells on the most dangerous and obnoxious events, recounting them in colorful detail. Consequently, while Mrs. Heartfree, as a paradigm of wifely virtue, should have foregone the pleasures of narration, Mrs. Heartfree the narrator actually and, in her own way, effectively rejoices in such pleasures.

A third significant interruption of Mrs. Heartfree's narrative reveals her vain delight in reporting the many romantic advances she suffered during the course of her travels. After a chapter-long disruption that deals with Wild's discovery of his own wife's infidelity, Mrs. Heartfree resumes her narrative by beginning to repeat compliments from one of her "admirers":

> 'If I mistake not, I was interrupted just as I was beginning to repeat some of the compliments made me by the hermit.'—'Just as you had finished them, I believe, madam,' said the justice.—'Very well, sir,' said she; 'I am sure I have no pleasure in the repetition. He concluded then with telling me, though I was in his eyes the most charming woman in the world, and might tempt a saint to abandon the ways of holiness, yet my beauty inspired him with a much tenderer affection towards me than to purchase any satisfaction of his own desires with my misery; if therefore I could be so cruel to him to reject his honest and sincere address, nor could submit to a solitary life with one who would endeavor by all possible means to make me happy, I had no force to dread; for that I was as much at my liberty as if I was in France, or England, or any other free country.'[16]

The long sentence that follows Mrs. Heartfree's assertion that she does not enjoy repeating the compliments the hermit had given her, of course, simply recapitulates them in considerable detail, and the entire construction of the humorous incident foregrounds the vanity that she expresses throughout her extensive narrative.

These three passages from *Jonathan Wild*, therefore, all reveal a conflict between Mrs. Heartfree's function in the satire as a paragon of wifely virtue and her activity as a narrator who, while attempting to narrate an effective narrative, reveals human frailty. Although the intrusive device that disrupts her narration is different in each of the three cases, all three examples of narrative disruption illustrate the pleasures Mrs. Heartfree derives from her performance, from, in short, the power her role as narrator gives her to impress her audience, as well as flatter her own vanity.[17] This ironic tension between Mrs. Heartfree's contradictory roles in *Jonathan Wild* clearly parallels the implications of the narrator's comments on the summarized narratives of both Tom and Sophia in *Tom Jones.* Narrating, it would seem, characterizes; it even humanizes, but, ironically, this very consequence threatens a narrator's existence as a stable paradigm because, once put into motion, conflict is necessarily introduced between that paradigm and all the various ambiguities of human action and motivation.

The comic unmasking of a character by the localized use of first-person narration does not appear to implicate the primary narrator in this limited context. Nonetheless, *Jonathan Wild* does offer an example where the ironic narrator draws explicit parallels between the arts of politics (or, in Fielding's word, "pollitrics") and the conventional duplicities involved in the literary arts.[18] The ironic narrator says of the great man that

> He doth indeed, in this grand drama, rather perform the part of the prompter, and doth instruct the well-dressed figures, who are strutting in public on the stage, what to say and do. To say the truth, a puppet-show will illustrate our meaning better, where it is the master of the show (the great man) who dances and moves everything, whether it be the king of Muscovy or whatever other potentate *alias* puppet which we behold on the stage; but he himself keeps wisely out of sight, for, should he once appear, the whole motion would be at an end.[19]

The ironic narrator continues by observing that the invisibility of the great mover is, in fact, only apparent because everyone knows of the great man's presence behind the scenes and because all agree "to be imposed upon."[20]

The narrator then develops his contention by claiming that "no one is ashamed of consenting to be imposed upon" and that, far from showing any

shame in the imposition, the compliant members of the public actually join
in the game

> of helping on the drama, by calling the several sticks
> or puppets by names which the master hath allotted
> to them, and by assigning to each the character which
> the great man is pleased they shall move in, or rather
> in which he himself is pleased to move them.[21]

The relationship between the great man and his audience is, in other words,
a reciprocal one, and, certainly, such an explanation of the fully conventional
nature of the relationship involves the audience in the great man's guilt.
Finally, perhaps the darkest implication of this particular theory of "pollitrics" is that the audience of the great man's puppet play appears to assume
some of the character of greatness, for, as the great man manipulates his
minions for his own gain, the audience itself allows (and even participates in)
the action until the individual members tire of that particular game. Then,
at least as in the case of Jonathan Wild, the great public audience sends its
great man to Tyburn Hill where he is literally made into a puppet who
dances one final dance for the public's edification.[22]

    In spite of such indications of the general public's culpability in the
career of greatness, the narrator further broadens his use of both high and
low drama to illustrate the machinations of greatness by including the readers
of romances in his developing figure:

> The truth is, they [the members of the audience] are
> in the same situation with the readers of romances;
> who, though they know the whole to be one entire
> fiction, nevertheless agree to be deceived; and, as
> these find amusement, so do the others find ease and
> convenience in this concurrence.[23]

Although the primary satiric thrust of these passages reveals the whole Punch
and Judy show of national politics, as well as the general character of

greatness, nevertheless, the figurative language employed cuts both ways. If the great man, whether a Walpole or an Alexander, is exposed by the satiric unmasking of the ironic text, along with the culpable audience that allows the political game to operate in the first place, then the implications of duplicity carry over to the metaphorical equivalents—dramatic productions and prose fictions. A narrator of any narrative becomes an example of greatness, a manipulator who controls characters in the manner of great politicians who direct their minions or puppet-masters who animate their marionettes to the tune of their own purposes. Narration is reduced to another species of "pollitrics," to another kind of game that, operating with a largely unspoken set of conventional rules, the great narrator and a compliant audience play in concert.

A further significance of these passages from *Jonathan Wild* that link narration to "pollitrics" comes from the fact that Fielding seems to be perfectly aware of what he is doing. He has, in other words, constructed a narrator who, in his turn, constructs a narrative that ironically reveals the inherent duplicity of the narrative act itself. Not only does he expose the complicity between reader and literary artist, but he implies that the relationship involves at least some of the unpleasantness of "pollitrics." Yet these comic condemnations of narrators and narration are just that—comic condemnations. They involve a good deal of high-spirited and sophisticated play with the game of narration, but they do not really offer a moral indictment of fiction in any serious Platonic manner that would expel poets from the ideal state. Rather, Fielding's comic play with the inherent self-interestedness and intentionality of narration predates Sterne's Lockean play in *Tristram Shandy*. As Sterne develops the relativity implicit in Locke's insistence that all human knowledge originates in experience and sensation, so Fielding implies the fundamental isolation of the individual human in his narrator's assertion that every first-person narration must be slanted toward the individual narrating the tale, although, of course, the narration may reveal rather than mask individual weaknesses.[24]

Moreover, the play with the narrative game implicates the narrator of *Tom Jones* himself because he too often speaks in the first person for his own rhetorical purposes. Certainly, the narrator's introductory chapters to each of the books are personal essays in which he narrates his ideas on narrative theory, the rights and privileges of authorship, critical injustice, and an entire range of similar subjects. His opening "Bill of Fare" implies a rather sordid monetary interest at the base of his "History." Likewise, the theory of selection maintained in the essays introducing the second and third books also implicates him in exactly the kind of interested selection that he criticizes in the summaries of both Tom's and Sophia's narratives and that he dramatically illustrates in the narrations of Mrs. Fitzpatrick and the Old Man of the Hill.

If such selectiveness is inherently duplicitous in any first-person narration, then the implications infect all narratives, and the important questions become those that inquire into the rhetoric that the narrator employs and his intentions in the application. For, given the human lack of any absolute knowledge, all narrative constructions must be mediated through the filter of the narrative voice. Consequently, the emphasis that Fielding's narrator in *Tom Jones* gives to his selectiveness ironically calls his own act of narration into question. By foregrounding his principle of selection, his method of inclusion and exclusion, the narrator objectifies the act of narration itself. His own choice of events of "Consequence" becomes a subject of inquiry. Indeed, this complex comic situation marks the master-stroke of Fielding the comic artist. Through his creation of narrators whose reflexive narrations disintegrate through their own reflexivity, he has created texts that not only play the game of narrative, as politicians play the game of control with a compliant audience, but that finally play a game of games that is complex, intelligent, and never-ending.

Notes

1. Ian Watt, *The Rise of the Novel: Studies in Defoe, Richardson, and Fielding* (Berkeley: U of California P, 1957) 30.

2. Watt 30.

3. Henry Fielding, Preface, *Joseph Andrews*, ed. Martin C. Battestin, *The Wesleyan Edition of the Works of Henry Fielding*, ex. ed. W. B. Coley (Middletown: Wesleyan UP, 1967) 4.

4. For a discussion of Jenny Cameron, see F. Homes Dudden, *Henry Fielding: His Life, Works, and Times*, vol. 1 (Hamden: Archon, 1966) 511–12.

5. Eric Rothstein argues that the narrator uses similar ploys to control the reader and to usurp narrative authority for himself. It seems, however, that the reader is meant to see through such patently obvious moves as the narrator's hostility in this introductory chapter. Indeed, the narrator's play for power undercuts his authority rather than enhances it. See Eric Rothstein, "Virtues of Authority in *Tom Jones*," *The Eighteenth Century: Theory and Interpretation* 28 (1987): 99–126.

6. The editors of the Wesleyan edition of *Tom Jones* point out that the lottery was a common satiric target for Fielding. See Fielding's ballad-opera *The Lottery* and his *Champion* essays for December 29, 1739, and January 3, 1739/40 (*Tom Jones* 1: 76–77n).

7. The inscription and punctuation of discourse that is grammatically indirect as if it were direct is a common trait of Fielding's prose. At times, this trait leads to interesting situations. In book 5, chapter 8, for example, the narrator has the Physician inquire of Thwackum and Square how the household is dealing with the supposed "final" illness of Mr. Allworthy and his generosity in his last will and testament: "The Physician now arrived, and began to enquire of the two Disputants, *How we all did above Stairs*?" (Fielding's emphasis, 1: 248). The italicized question, which marks the grammatical confusion between direct and indirect discourse turns on the ambiguous *we*, for the pronoun reference seems to imply that the narrator himself was present in the scene. However, to push a small point so far would no doubt be pushing too far. Although Michael Irwin has used this characteristic confusion between direct and indirect quotation in his criticism of Fielding's narrative methods, the most obvious answer is that Fielding is here employing his equally characteristic allowance to doctors and lawyers to speak in their own voices. In short, he seems to conceive of the physician coming in and saying in a typical bedside manner, "Well, and how are *we* doing this morning?" See Michael Irwin, *Henry Fielding: The Tentative Realist* (Oxford: Clarendon, 1967) 101.

8. This discrepancy can be accounted for by the motivation of self-interest. Partridge believes that Tom has run away from Mr. Allworthy and Paradise Hall, and he hopes that he can be reinstated in Allworthy's good graces by convincing Tom to return. In contrast, not only do the other narratives in *Tom Jones* that Partridge continually interrupts awaken

his fear of the supernatural, but also a good audience would require a stepping outside of his rather limited personal point of view. In fact, his interruptions are marked by their concern for personal safety and well-being.

9. E. M. Forster, *Aspects of the Novel* (New York: Harvest, 1955) 26, 27–28.

10. Forster 86. The Russian Formalists made a similar distinction between the *fabula*, or "the chronological sequence of events," and the *syuzhet*, or "the order and manner in which they are actually presented in the narrative." They argued that "the *syuzhet* creates a defamiliarizing effect on the *fabula*." Ann Jefferson, "Russian Formalism," *Modern Literary Theory: A Comparative Introduction*, ed. Ann Jefferson and David Robey (Totowa: Barnes & Noble, 1982) 31. See also Terry Eagleton, *Literary Theory: An Introduction* (Minneapolis: U of Minnesota P, 1983) 105. For an example of a Formalist's treatment of eighteenth-century British fiction, see Victor Shklovsky, "Sterne's *Tristram Shandy*: Stylistic Commentary," *Russian Formalist Criticism: Four Essays*, trans. Lee T. Lemon and Marion J. Reis. Regents Critics Series, gen. ed. Paul A. Olson (Lincoln: U of Nebraska P, 1965) 25–57.

11. See book 8, chapters 11–15, for the Old Man of the Hill's narration (1: 451–86).

12. Mrs. Fitzpatrick's narration follows a pattern that is characteristic of Fielding's narrative method—that of narrative interruption. She narrates her own tale through the course of three different chapters: book 11, chapters 4, 5, and 7. Chapter 6, however, deals with the landlord's interruption with news of the progress of the rebellion. In his turn, Partridge continually interrupts the narration of the Old Man of the Hill in book 8. This pattern of interruption recalls the Russian Formalists' distinction between *syuzhet* and *fabula*. This pattern of disruption in local narratives parallels the larger structural principle of narrative interruption controlling the development of *Tom Jones* itself.

13. For Joseph's letters, see Henry Fielding, *Joseph Andrews* 31–32, 46–47.

14. Henry Fielding, *The History of the Life of the Late Mr. Jonathan Wild*, vol. 2 of *The Complete Works of Henry Fielding, Esq.*, ed. William Ernest Henley (1903; New York: Barnes & Noble, 1967) 166–67.

15. Henry Fielding, *Jonathan Wild* 169.

16. Henry Fielding, *Jonathan Wild* 183–84.

17. Michael McKeon maintains that Mrs. Heartfree's use of romance conventions allows the reader to question the validity of her assertion that she had been faithful to her husband throughout her adventures. For McKeon's arguments, see *The Origins of the English Novel, 1600–1740* (Baltimore: Johns Hopkins UP, 1987) 390–92.

18. Fielding's ironic narrator of *Jonathan Wild* offers a clear definition of "pollitrics":
    With such infinite address did this truly great man know how

to play with the passions of men, to set them at variance with each other, and to work his own purposes out of those jealousies and apprehensions which he was wonderfully ready at creating by means of those great arts which the vulgar call treachery, dissembling, promising, lying, falsehood, etc., but which are by great men summed up in the collective name of policy, or politics, or rather pollitrics; an art of which, as it is the highest excellence of human nature, perhaps our great man was the most eminent master. (73)

It is of considerable importance that this statement is closely followed by an example of the great man's oratory, of, in other words, his rhetorical cookery employed for the maintenance of power. See chapter 6, book 2, "*Of hats*" (73–75).

19. Henry Fielding, *Jonathan Wild* 131.

20. Henry Fielding, *Jonathan Wild* 131. Fielding's narrator emphasizes these passages by the title of the chapter in which they occur: "*A scheme so deeply laid, that it shames all the politics of this our age; with digression and subdigression.*" Given the persistent parallels between "pollitrics" and the literary arts, the deeply laid scheme appears to be the narrative game itself. The notice given to the digression and subdigression in the title marks a typical example of Fieldingesque misdirection, for what is labeled marginal actually treats the issues.

21. Henry Fielding, *Jonathan Wild* 131.

22. For a discussion of capital punishment in eighteenth-century England, see Frank McLynn, *Crime and Punishment in Eighteenth-century England* (Oxford: Oxford UP, 1991) 257–76.

23. Henry Fielding, *Jonathan Wild* 132.

24. John Preston points out that Fielding recognized a relationship between his text and Locke's *Essay*. Preston also quotes an important passage from Fielding's *Champion* essay from March 1, 1739/40, in which, after quoting Locke on how the eye does not see itself as an object of contemplation except with "*Art and Pains*," Fielding writes that "the Eye can contemplate itself in a Glass, but no *Narcissus* hath hitherto discovered any Mirrour for the Understanding...." Preston correctly concludes that *Tom Jones* is such a mirror. John Preston, *The Created Self: The Reader's Role in Eighteenth-Century Fiction* (London: Heinemann, 1970) 117. Also see Henry Fielding, "Articles in the *Champion*," vol. 15 of *The Complete Works of Henry Fielding, Esq.*, ed. William Ernest Henley (1903; New York: Barnes & Noble, 1967) 223.

CHAPTER
4

A Rhetoric of Deception:
The Characterization of Bridget Allworthy

> *'I should not believe such a story were it told me by Cato'* was
> *a proverbial saying in Rome, even during the lifetime of that*
> *philosophical patriot.*
>
> David Hume

Samuel Taylor Coleridge's well-known designation of the plot of *Tom Jones*
as one of "the three most perfect plots ever planned" most certainly isolates
an important element of Fielding's text.[1] The plot of *Tom Jones* is, indeed,
remarkably well planned.   Yet Coleridge's assessment also grants the plot
undue emphasis, precipitating it out of its complex narrative nexus.   Plot
assumes an importance, a self-sufficiency even, that diminishes the other
elements and distorts the compound relationships of the text. Nevertheless,
enlarging upon Coleridge's assessment, considerable critical discourse has
been concerned with Fielding's architectural prowess, with, in a word, the
design of *Tom Jones*. Dorothy Van Ghent and Frederick W. Hilles have, for
example, both compared *Tom Jones* to a "Palladian palace."[2]   Widely
disseminated through quotation, such readings of the thematic significance of
the shape and symmetry of *Tom Jones* have come to support the entire
critical complex that interprets the text as a providential comedy.

Arguments of significant design assert that the symmetry of the
"Palladian" plot of *Tom Jones* reflects Fielding's assurance of an equally
symmetrical universal order and, furthermore, that his comedic resolution of
the various complications of the plot mirrors the theoretical operations of a

beneficent providence in the larger world beyond the text. In this view, the plot of *Tom Jones* becomes an assertion of epiphany, and the ironic narrator, a textual representative of the divine plot-maker.[3] Ignoring the duplicity of the narrator's characteristic use of ironic misdirection, the proponents of these providential arguments further obscure the issue by naïvely identifying the narrator of *Tom Jones* with the actual author, the historical Henry Fielding himself. The witty, sophisticated, and benevolent Justice from Bow Street becomes for many such critics the trustworthy and benevolent narrator of the text:[4] Yet to make these thematic associations between the narrator and providence, a reader must patently ignore the fundamental irony that the narrator can only achieve the completion of his orderly and symmetrical "Palladian palace" through a consistent use of a rhetoric of deception that for much of the text actively fosters misconception.[5]

The narrator's apparent benevolence and his consummate skill in conducting the reversals of the plot are both compromised by the elementary fact that he can only construct the "Palladian" plot that he constructs by a practiced deception. He must maintain the cardinal secret of Tom's parentage if he is to achieve his comic reversal after his hero has reached a nadir from which there appears to be no escape but the gallows. The narrator cannot allow the reader (during, of course, a first reading) to guess the pertinent facts of Tom's birth before he reveals the truth in accordance with his plan.[6] The narrator is obliged to deceive his readers, to misdirect them. By using such devices as the false confession and erroneous conviction of Jenny Jones, the narrator actually hides the fact that the circumstances of Tom's birth are open to question. To be sure, even readers who have only a limited knowledge of comic conventions will expect some sudden change in the fortunes of the hero, but the important point is that, for all of his intrusive openness, the narrator of *Tom Jones* consistently employs rhetoric that directs readers away from Tom's origins. This persistent deception undermines the narrator's alleged objectivity by revealing the motivation behind his narrative selection and, at the same time, seriously complicates any incipient analogue between him and a benevolent providence through the implications of an active hypocrisy.

Because of the particular design of his birth-mystery plot, the narrator is actually forced to ally himself with several of the more dubious characters in *Tom Jones* during the course of his narration. As Bridget Allworthy and her maid, Jenny Jones, conspire to deceive Mr. Allworthy about the facts surrounding the foundling's birth, so the narrator must conspire to deceive his readers since Tom's secret heritage functions as the keystone of his complicated design. With more sinister overtones, the narrator is obligated by the design of his plot to conceal Bridget's letter that contains her death-bed confession from the reader as Blifil and his confederate, the lawyer Dowling, are obligated by their own intrigues to conceal the said letter from Allworthy. Like Blifil, the narrator can only complete his own elaborate plot by hiding Bridget's text. Additionally, since his narrative plan presupposes a retrospective narration and his consequent knowledge of the resolution, the narrator must persuade his readers that Bridget's character flaws, her motives, and even her hypocrisies are other than his knowledge of the events shows them to be.

Deception, therefore, controls the narrator's characterization of Bridget Allworthy. Since the narrator must manipulate the reader's response if he is to complete his plot successfully, he must devise a deceptive rhetoric that obscures the facts in the case until he is ready to reveal the secret upon which his plot is founded. Obligated to deceive his readers by obscuring the evidence of Bridget's maternal relation to Tom, the narrator exploits the reader's reliance on conventional social and literary types to decode texts. In particular, he exploits the common comic type of the sexually frustrated spinster in his characterization of Bridget Allworthy to mislead his readers, using the conventionalized expectations implicit in the type to help maintain his secret.

The logical consequences of such a pervasive irony indicate that the resolution of the various conflicts in *Tom Jones* does not placidly reflect a cosmic order signaled by the complacent assurance of a "Palladian" design. Rather, the text of *Tom Jones* appears to offer a comic exploration of the contradictions implicit in such a providential order or, at least, in the limited human understanding and articulation of that order. Given the narrator's deceptive methods, that is, given the fundamental conflict between the orderly design of the plot and the deceptive rhetoric that the narrator must employ to achieve the completion of that design, the emphasis is shifted from a self-assured assertion of a special cosmic benevolence working secretly to bring everything to rights toward a devious—but nevertheless comic—inquiry into the inadequacy of human understanding.

The narrator's application of deceptive rhetoric in the characterization of Bridget begins with his introduction of both her brother, Mr. Allworthy, and herself in the second chapter of the first book, "*A short Description of Squire* Allworthy, *and a fuller Account of Miss* Bridget Allworthy *his Sister.*" The immediate irony of this chapter title is that there is nothing "*fuller,*" nothing more complete, about the opening maneuvers in the narrator's characterization of Bridget. Employing the misdirection implicit in the use of the conventional type of the comic spinster, even the narrator's opening insistence on the ambiguous *Miss* in the chapter title misdirects the reader and obscures the motivation behind Bridget's actions. For, although *Miss* could signify a mistress, concubine, or prostitute in the eighteenth century, it is likely that, given the context of Allworthy's Paradise Hall and the narrator's following character of the woman in question, readers would favor the equally possible meaning of *Miss* as a title signifying an unmarried woman for whom *Lady* or some other indication of higher rank would not have been appropriate.[7] The important point here is that, while a reader with knowledge of the narrator's secret would be able to note the ironic implications about Bridget's sexual behavior implicit in the narrator's introduction of her name into the text, certainly most readers would readily accept *Miss* as an indication of Bridget's unmarried status on first reading.

Following this gambit, the narrator quickly moves to the initial characterization of Allworthy and Bridget in the four paragraphs of chapter 2, book 1. He describes Allworthy in the first two, and then he follows this description of the brother with his so-called "*fuller Account*" of the sister in the third (1: 34–35, 35–37). In the final paragraph of the chapter, the narrator informs the reader of his intention of continual intrusion into the narrative whenever he deems it necessary (1: 37). The mere juxtaposition of the deceptive introduction of Bridget in such close proximity to the narrator's assertion of his narrative bill of rights aids in the necessary deception. On an initial reading, the narrator's open and easy discussion of his methods functions to disguise the rhetorical manipulation, to enhance, in other words, the reader's belief in his apparent truthfulness and reliability. Only on a second reading can the narrator's sophistic moves be noted (and fully appreciated by the reader) for what they are.

Furthermore, the purely physical evidence of the print on the page belies the narrator's assertion about the completeness of his initial treatment of Bridget. In fact, the *"fuller Account"* of Bridget Allworthy is actually shorter than the account given of her brother. While the narrator's opening description of Bridget runs for 312 words, his initial treatment of Allworthy is 326 words long. It would appear that the narrator's joke at the reader's expense here involves the physical fact that the so-called *"fuller Account"* is actually shorter than the account that the narrator identifies as less complete. Although a raw word count will never identify the completeness and reliability of any passage, the narrator's plot demands that he convince the reader that in Bridget's case less is more, that she is a shallow character, flat and easily comprehended, incapable of any surprising secret. Consequently, in this first mention of Bridget in the title of book 1, chapter 2, the narrator implies that his quick sketch of her character contains what is basically a complete accounting of the essential facts.

In the account itself, the narrator presents Bridget as the typical comic spinster, embittered and frustrated, with only those stock hypocrisies expected of the type:

> He [Allworthy] now lived, for the most Part, retired
> in the Country, with one Sister, for whom he had a
> very tender Affection. This Lady was now somewhat
> past the Age of 30, an Æra, at which, in the Opinion
> of the malicious, the Title of Old Maid may, with no
> Impropriety, be assumed. She was of that Species of
> Women, whom you commend rather for good Quali-
> ties than Beauty, and who are generally called by

their own Sex, very good Sort of Women—as good a
Sort of Woman, Madam, as you would wish to know.
(1: 35—36)

Highly ironic and oblique, this description directs the reader more toward the
generic than to the individual. Bridget is of the age that evokes the stock
response of the commonly malicious—"Old Maid." Not individualized as a
particular example of feminine existence, Bridget is "of that Species of
Women" who appear rather good than beautiful. She is considered a "very
good Sort" by other women because they do not perceive her as a sexual
threat. The narrator parrots the standard conclusion of a typical public
judgment: "as good a Sort of Woman, Madam, as you would wish to know."
Every detail of this initial picture of Bridget leads away from her cardinal
secret and directs the reader toward a stock response. Paradoxically, even
a reading that recognizes the ironic criticism of hasty judgments based on an
uncritical application of established types indicated by the narrator's language
reinforces the implication that Bridget's character conforms to the conventional characteristics of the type.

The narrator continues his deceptive linking of Bridget to the comic
type of the frustrated and embittered spinster in the following sentence:

Indeed she was so far from regretting Want of
Beauty, that she never mention'd that Perfection (if
it can be called one) without some Contempt; and
would often thank God she was not as handsome as
Miss such a one, whom perhaps Beauty had led into
Errors, which she might have otherwise avoided.
Miss *Bridget Allworthy* (for that was the Name of this
Lady) very rightly conceived the Charms of Person in
a Woman to be no better than Snares for herself, as
well as for others, and yet so discreet was she in her
Conduct, that her Prudence was as much on the
Guard, as if she had all the Snares to apprehend
which were ever laid for her whole Sex. (1: 36—37)

The full irony of this description, of course, is only available on a second reading, for, given her own want of beauty, Bridget's disdain for physical charms seems to be motivated by her jealousy of others rather than by a knowing discretion. Unlike such notorious Restoration examples as Lady Wishfort or Mrs. Loveit, Bridget's prudish behavior appears on first acquaintance to be motivated by an envious hostility toward all females who have either found physical satisfaction in the opposite sex or whose appearance attracts male attention. Her prudish litany of endangered virtue seems to spring from her own failure in the sexual game and to be powered by an inverted wish-fulfillment.

The narrator's rhetorical misdirection is further illustrated by the next sentence, a generalization on the battle of the sexes that he validates by his own experience and supports with a military figure:

> Indeed, I have observed (tho' it may seem unaccountable to the Reader) that this Guard of Prudence, like the Trained Bands, is always readiest to go on Duty where there is the least Danger. It often basely and cowardly deserts those Paragons for whom the Men are all wishing, sighing, dying, and spreading every Net in their Power; and constantly attends at the Heels of that higher Order of Women, for whom the other Sex have a more distant and awful Respect, and whom (from Despair, I suppose, of Success) they never venture to attack. (1: 37)

The narrator's caustic wit here reinforces the deception in the previous elements of the paragraph. No beauty herself, Bridget rationalizes her lack of physical charms into a blessing, and, consequently, she appears to be a recognizable member of that prudent "higher Order of Women" who expend their frustrated sexual energy in defending that which needs no defense. Even his ludicrous parenthetical supposition implies the shallow reading of Bridget's character that the narrator must foster upon the reader if he is to maintain the secret essential to his plot. Men, the narrator surmises, fail to approach such women of the "higher Order," not from an actual fear of rejection but rather because such women are sexually unattractive. There is also a possible, if somewhat distant, implication in the word *success* that indicates the potential failure of sexual desire if a man were to engage such prudent women whom men "never venture to attack." Unpleasant, even harsh in the ironic convolution, such implications all work to forestall any possible connection between Bridget and sexual attraction, forestalling, as a consequence, the possibility of any serious suspicion of a blood relation between the comely, warm-hearted Tom and his actual mother, Bridget.

With innuendo, misdirection, and outright deception, therefore, the narrator works his sophistic "Cookery." He appeals to the conventional characterization of the comic spinster to entrap the reader in a reflex reaction. By encoding his passage with the traditional age of "somewhat past the Age of 30," by parroting the commonplace voice of the "malicious," and by assigning Bridget the conventional hypocritical virtue of the frustrated spinster, the narrator offers the reader a plausible motivation for Bridget's actions. Even a sophisticated reader has little more than the marked lack of exact detail in this *"fuller Account"* and the generally indirect nature of the comments to identify the narrator's deception at first sight. Such a reader may recognize the conventional hypocrisy of Bridget's position, but the conventional frustration and desperation of an unwilling spinster clearly can account for her peevish unpleasantness.

Of course, such an interpretation is exactly the position that the narrator is obligated to force upon his readers. Consequently, he echoes the established assumptions expressed by the common public voice in his initial description of Bridget Allworthy. He later develops his use of the signal phrase "somewhat past the Age of 30," which mimics the conventional reluctance of generic spinsters to reveal their age, in chapter 8 of book 1, revealing that Bridget has actually approached the age of forty (1: 56).[8] By insisting that Bridget is a member of a readily recognizable "Species" rather than an individual woman, that she is, in other words, an example of "that higher Order of Women" whom men only regard with "awful Respect," the narrator prevents the possibility of any serious connection between Bridget and sexual attraction, slyly directing his readers toward understanding her in the standard conventional terms as a character lacking in the depth for anything but the thoroughly conventional hypocrisy normally associated with the comic type.

The case could be made that the narrator's appeal to such generalized characterization is primarily an example of the characteristic neoclassical move toward generic classification, another example, in short, of Imlac's famous tulip. Still, the narrator's use of this standard principle of neoclassical poetics does in fact further his rhetorical purposes. His failure to individualize Bridget with particular and individual streaks of her own, although standard neoclassical practice, also indicates his exploitation of the literary conventions and predictable habits of thought that would determine his reader's understanding of the text. In the final analysis, *Tom Jones* may be read as an actual assault on the easy complacency that can result from such a habitual reliance on types. Indeed, Tom's own illegitimacy functions to illustrate the manifest injustice that springs from a reflex judgment based solely on the prejudicial use of simplistic types.

In book 18, chapter 10, for example, Squire Western's sudden change in behavior illustrates the case when he addresses Tom after learning the truth of Tom's parentage:

> *Western* immediately went up to *Jones*, crying out, 'My old Friend *Tom*, I am glad to see thee with all my Heart. All past must be forgotten. I could not intend any Affront to thee, because, as *Allworthy* here knows, nay, dost know it thyself, I took thee for another Person; and where a Body means no Harm, what signifies a hasty Word or two; one Christian must forget and forgive another.' (2: 963)

Beyond the *non sequitur* in Squire Western's argument, his assertion that he had previously taken Tom "for another Person" reveals the intellectual—to say nothing of the moral—shortcomings of an uncritical and judgmental use of overly simplistic paradigms. Squire Western had known and loved the young Tom as a sporting lad who excelled in the pleasures of the field. Yet, as the beggarly, bastard son of the maid Jenny Jones and the schoolmaster Partridge, Tom was not the type of young man that Western could accept as a suitable match for either his daughter, Sophia, or his country estate. However, once Squire Western learns of Tom's newly revealed identity, he quickly revises his opinion of the young upstart. Immediately rejecting the now disgraced Blifil as a fitting match for his daughter, Western calls Tom "as hearty an honest Cock as any in the Kingdom" and desires to lead him to Sophia, quickly redirecting his old pursuit of the many benefits of marrying his own heir to the heir of Allworthy's neighboring Paradise Hall.

Such a passage foregrounds the shortcomings of both Squire Western's character and the social "understandings" that degrade marriage into merely a monetary enterprise. Western did not initially reject Tom as a fitting son-in-law because he was a bastard but rather because he was only a poor one. Nevertheless, Fielding does not completely transform his foundling frog into a perfect young prince. In contrast to the conventional circumstances of the nativity of Joseph Andrews, Tom's birth remains "dubious." For Squire Western, Tom may be suitably legitimized by his blood-relation to Mr. Allworthy, but, for the reader, the legitimization of Tom largely derives from his various actions illustrating his fundamental goodness of heart and not from the mere accident of his birth. Western's unambiguous type of the suitable young gentleman of birth is, therefore, complicated and its limitations revealed. The standard for judgment is shifted from a clear and stable, although simplistic, paradigm toward the more ambiguous standard of action, and the definition of a suitable young man shifts from one who is well-born toward one who acts well.

Ironically, however, this broadening of the limits of type that the narrator develops throughout the text in his treatment of Tom is directly opposed by his treatment of Bridget. With her characterization, the narrator's deceptive method functions by misdirecting the reader toward preconceived notions based on assumptions and conventions, on, that is, the standard type of the comic spinster. The unmasking of Blifil's villainy, the discovery of Bridget's secret, and the revelation of Allworthy's own unwitting injustice during the climactic scenes of the text also unmask the reader's own intellectual pride. As Blifil, Bridget, Thwackum, and Square all work to deceive Allworthy, so the narrator works with his rhetorical deception to entrap the reader and to illustrate dramatically the shortfall of humanity's intellectual tools.

This game of rhetorical entrapment initiated in the introduction of Bridget is continued and further complicated by the report the narrator gives of her reaction to the discovery of the infant Tom in Mr. Allworthy's bedchamber. After Mr. Allworthy has announced his discovery to his sister, Mrs. Wilkins's expectations of a violent outburst of indignant "Virtue" from Bridget are disappointed:

> Miss *Bridget* had always exprest so great a regard for what the Ladies are pleased to call Virtue, and had herself maintained such a Severity of Character, that it was expected, especially by *Wilkins*, that she would have vented much Bitterness on this Occasion, and would have voted for sending the Child, as a kind of noxious Animal, immediately out of the House; but on the contrary, she rather took the good-natur'd side of the question, intimated some Compassion for the helpless little Creature, and commended her Brother's Charity in what he had done. (1: 44)

Bridget's motivation for what Mrs. Wilkins perceives as her compassion might well be maternal since her plot is designed to dupe her brother into adopting her own illegitimate son. The narrator must, like Bridget, disguise the essential facts in the case; consequently, he offers the reader a possible motivation that is suitable to his deceptive purposes. He speculates that Bridget's kindness toward "the helpless little Creature" might be explained by her position in Allworthy's household. "Perhaps the Reader," the narrator suggests, "may account for this Behaviour from her Condescension to Mr. *Allworthy*..." (1: 44). He reinforces his misleading supposition by pointing out that Bridget would often bow to the wishes of her brother, although "she would indeed sometimes make a few Observations, as, that Men were headstrong and must have their own way, and would wish she had been blest with an independent Fortune..." (1: 45).

Neatly covering Bridget's maternal interest in the issue with his deceptive speculation, the narrator continues to direct the reader toward understanding Bridget as only the typical spinster. Her taking "the good-natur'd side of the question" is, however, an actual necessity and not merely a kindness. As a dependent and a poor relation, a suffering sister without the independence of her own fortune, Bridget has often had to bend to what the narrator implies she sees as the strange whims of a headstrong male. Only after a complete reading of the text does the irony of the narrator's comment on Bridget's knowledge of the willfulness of men become apparent. Bridget does know what it means to have to deal with the headstrong male, to have, in short, the young Mr. Summer have his own way with her. Although such a description of the relationship between Bridget and Mr. Summer would, no doubt, be more of a rationalization on Bridget's part than an objective description, the fact remains that the narrator misdirects the first-time reader in the passage by obscuring Bridget's motivation. The narrator's supposition on the cause of her apparent kindness toward "the helpless little Creature" leads the reader to interpret her act of compassion as an obligation and as further evidence of her status as an old maid living with a rich brother.

Beyond such indirect reporting of Bridget's "Muttering," the narrator strengthens his deceptive description of Bridget as a typical example of the frustrated spinster by summarizing her opinion of the "unknown" mother of little Tom:

> However, what she withheld from the Infant, she bestowed with the utmost Profuseness on the poor unknown Mother, whom she called an impudent Slut, a wanton Hussy, an audacious Harlot, a wicked Jade, a vile Strumpet, with every other Appellation with which the Tongue of Virtue never fails to lash those who bring a Disgrace on the Sex. (1: 45)

Bridget's hostility here appears on first reading to be another example of the standard hypocrisy of conventional prudishness. Although it implies that Bridget's "Virtue" is suspect, the final clause—"which the Tongue of Virtue never fails to lash those who bring a Disgrace on the Sex"—in fact recalls the descent into the Cave of Spleen from the fourth canto of Pope's *Rape of the Lock* and those "scornful virgins who their charms survive."[9] On a second reading, however, after a complete knowledge of Bridget's secret has been gained, this report of Bridget's abusive language becomes highly ambiguous. She could be simply playing a part to cover her sexual indiscretion, but she could also be heaping a very real abuse upon herself as an ironic form of atonement.

The gap between the flat, ludicrous Bridget of a first reading and the more complex and even pathetic Bridget of subsequent readings indicates the degree of the narrator's rhetorical manipulation. His rhetoric flattens Bridget's character. It belies the considerable complexity of her real motivation; indeed, it could be argued that her act has elements of a certain selflessness. It is true that she is culpable for her inability simply to admit her circumstances to her brother and reveal the young consequence. In all probability, such an act of open repentance would have gained Tom a secure maintenance. Nevertheless, Bridget is apparently unable to abandon her child completely, and she attempts to manipulate her brother at some danger to her own personal well-being since she cannot be absolutely certain how her brother would react if he were to discover her attempt to foster her own infant upon him. Surely, her intrigue reveals a clever awareness of Mr. Allworthy's self-assured complacence in his own benevolence, as well as the ability to take advantage of such knowledge. Her maneuvers imply a certain degree of limited, if somewhat misdirected, courage. But the narrator never grants either courage or cleverness to Bridget. He consistently paints her as a flat, conventional manikin rather than as a woman who has suffered both profound loss and deep personal crisis.

The narrator continues his rhetoric of misdirection in the next chapter, *"Containing a few common Matters, with a very uncommon Observation upon them."* Here he reports Bridget's response to her brother's request to prepare a nursery and other necessities for the mysterious infant, and in doing so, the narrator comes perilously close to an actual lie:

> Her Orders [to Wilkins] were indeed so liberal, that had it been a Child of her own, she could not have exceeded them; but lest the virtuous Reader may condemn her for shewing too great Regard to a base-born Infant, to which all Charity is condemned by Law as irreligious, we think proper to observe, that she concluded the whole with saying, 'Since it was her Brother's Whim to adopt the little Brat, she supposed little Master must be treated with great Tenderness; for her part, she could not help thinking it was an Encouragement to Vice; but she knew too much of the Obstinacy of Mankind to oppose any of their ridiculous Humours.' (1: 46)

Although the narrator's ironic rationalization to "the virtuous Reader" signals insincerity, the implication is that the narrator parodies the common voice of the maliciously "virtuous." The obvious irony of the comment on the impiety of charity to bastards emphasizes the satiric point. Indeed, the narrator's report of Bridget's comments to Wilkins about the "ridiculous Humours" of obstinate males merely completes the move.

Yet it is at this point that a reader could well question why Bridget does any more for the "little Brat" than is strictly necessary. Consequently, it is here that the narrator comes as close as he ever does to an outright assertion that Tom is not Bridget's child. Although ambiguous, the narrator's assertion that Bridget's orders could not have been more liberal "had it been a Child of her own" is a masterful example of misdirection. Certainly, such a phrase will be understood as a negation in normal usage. Readers will almost assuredly construe such a phrase to mean that, although the child is not her own, she could not have behaved more liberally had it been. The narrator plays with the codes of negation in English, exploiting the ambiguity. He does not deny that the infant is Bridget's, but he knows that the reader, following the standard grammar of negation in English, will understand his observation as such a negative.

A similar pattern of deception is repeated by the narrator in the eighth chapter of book 1, *"A Dialogue between Mesdames* Bridget, *and* Deborah *containing more Amusement, but less Instruction than the former."* This chapter title obviously links the chapter with the preceding one. Entitled *"Containing such grave Matter, that the Reader cannot laugh once through the whole Chapter, unless peradventure he should laugh at the Author,"* chapter 7 of book 1 deals with Allworthy's prosecution of Jenny Jones. Playing on the traditional Horatian justification of entertainment and enlightenment, the narrator's ironic chapter titles function to reinforce the erroneous understanding of the character of Bridget. His self-deprecating comment on his own high seriousness in the narration of Jenny's trial ironically enhances Allworthy's moralizing on the social and religious consequences of sexual misconduct, lending credence to the proceedings.

The humorous title given to chapter 8, on the other hand, deflates the important fact of Bridget's considerable interest in the outcome of Jenny's trial. The actions and dialogue of Bridget and Deborah Wilkins are branded as merely ridiculous, the stuff of mere amusement rather than the serious matter of respectable instruction. This sophistic maneuver in the narrator's rhetoric involves him in deception that parallels the intrigue that Bridget and Jenny have contrived to trick Mr. Allworthy on the score of Tom's parentage. As Allworthy is manipulated by his sister into convicting the wrong sinner, so the narrator once again manipulates the reader with his humorous chapter titles. His contrast between the instruction of the trial and the entertainment of the following ludicrous scene appears to validate Allworthy's "justice." The misleading information given during Jenny's hearing is enhanced, while the important hints about Bridget's secret interest in the event are obscured.

With *"A Dialogue,"* the narrator continues the consistent misrepresentation of Bridget as merely a conventional frustrated and embittered old virgin. After reporting that Bridget and Wilkins had positioned themselves in the room adjoining Allworthy's study so that they could listen to the proceedings through a convenient keyhole, the narrator offers an apparently ludicrous comparison between Bridget and Thisbe:

> This Hole in her Brother's Study Door, was indeed as well known to Miss *Bridget*, and had been as frequently applied to by her, as the famous Hole in the Wall was by *Thisbe* of old. This served to many good Purposes. For by such Means Miss *Bridget* became often acquainted with her Brother's Inclinations, without giving him the Trouble of repeating them to her. It is true, some Inconveniences attended this Intercourse and she had sometimes Reason to cry out with *Thisbe*, in *Shakespear*, 'O wicked, wicked Wall!' For as Mr. *Allworthy* was a Justice of Peace, certain Things occurred in Examinations concerning Bastards, and such like, which are apt to give great Offence to the chaste Ears of Virgins, especially when they approach the Age of forty, as was the Case of Miss *Bridget*. (1: 55−56)

Clearly, this passage is deceptive. Although not a direct assertion about Bridget's status, the last sentence certainly more than implies that Bridget was a virgin of approximately forty years of age at the time of the hearing. Nonetheless, the implications of the extended comparison to Thisbe offer an even richer network of ironic allusions.

Such an inappropriate comparison may be termed inverted wit, for the witty play lies in the inappropriateness of the figure contrary to Addison's dictates of multileveled comparison in his *Spectator* series on false wit.[10] Indeed, the comparison between the aging "virgin" and the fresh, young, and tragic lover appears ludicrous, even grotesque. The narrator's apparent witlessness in the inappropriateness of the comparison, however, slyly reinforces the characterization of Bridget as a ridiculous figure. Furthermore, the narrator's development of the comparison with the allusion, not to Ovid's serious treatment, but to Shakespeare's travesty of the old story

through the comic mechanics from *A Midsummer's Night's Dream* enhances
the rhetorical process. Since Bridget is neither young nor beautiful, the narrator's extended simile implies that she is the reverse of Thisbe on many
different levels. The implication to be drawn from the inaccurate comparison
is that Bridget could have no Pyramus, that she could interest no male as
Thisbe did. By a further extension, the narrator's inappropriate comparison
suggests that, as an example of the traditional comic spinster, Bridget, unlike
the young, tragic Thisbe, could have had nothing of serious or tragic consequence happen to her in the past. Bridget loses by the comparison. She
appears, in other words, to be every bit as ludicrous as Shakespeare's
dramatic mechanics, and, if she is not literally crowned with an ass's head,
she is, nonetheless, made to appear as ridiculous as Bottom and his friends
seem in their attempt to dramatize the tragic tale to the Athenian court.

In addition to these complications, by asserting that Bridget often makes
use of the keyhole as a useful listening post, the narrator lessens the
importance of this one specific instance. Bridget, he implies, has no
particular interest in Jenny's trial other than a vindictive curiosity, for she
makes a habit of eavesdropping on Allworthy's proceedings. Yet, as the
reader learns by the end of *Tom Jones*, Bridget is indeed vitally interested in
Jenny's evidence and the hoodwinking of her brother, the Justice. When the
narrator remarks that Bridget "discomposed her Features with a smile (a
Thing very unusual to her)" (1: 56), the first-time reader will almost certainly
interpret this smile as vindictive, vicious, and, indeed, triumphant, not because
of the success of her intrigue, but rather because another woman's sexual
satisfaction has been discovered and punished.

The use of the verb *discomposed*, along with the parenthetical assertion
on the rarity of Bridget's smile, signals to a reader the grotesque nature of
Bridget's facial change. In fact, the narrator develops this idea that Bridget's
smile was anything but pleasant:

> Not that I would have my Reader imagine, that this
> was one of those wanton Smiles, which *Homer* would
> have you conceive came from *Venus*, when he calls

> her the laughter-loving Goddess; nor was it one of
> those Smiles, which Lady *Seraphina* shoots from the
> Stage-Box, and which *Venus* would quit her Immor-
> tality to be able to equal. No, this was rather one of
> those Smiles, which might be supposed to have come
> from the dimpled Cheeks of the august *Tysiphone*, or
> from one of the Misses her Sisters. (1: 56)

Bridget's smile was a Fury's smile, and Bridget herself, "one of the Misses
her Sisters." Playing on the extended meaning of *Fury*, the narrator implies
that Bridget, like her mythological archetypes, avenges crime and thrills at
the suffering of the criminal. In addition, this linking of Bridget to the
Furies recalls the narrator's previous summary of Bridget's castigation of "the
poor unknown Mother" of young Tom, indicating that Bridget is truly adept
in the ready application of the "Tongue of Virtue" that "never fails to lash
those who bring a Disgrace on the Sex" (1: 45).

The narrator complicates his misdirection in the passage by contrasting
Bridget's smile to the lovely smiles of Lady Seraphina and Venus herself.
Such a maneuver once again separates Bridget from sexual attraction.
Unlike those women whose "wanton Smiles" rival the smile of Venus,
Bridget's bitter change of facial expression links her to punishment, not
sexual pleasure. To be sure, Bridget must have been embittered by the
result of her liaison with young Mr. Summer, for his death from smallpox left
her alone, unmarried, and pregnant. Nevertheless, apparent vengefulness
toward Jenny Jones hardly explains her reaction to the success of her plot to
find a safe haven for her illegitimate son. Certainly, Bridget's smile is one
of bitter irony, perhaps even of self-castigation. Still, her intrigue has
succeeded. Jenny has been as good as her word to perjure herself, and Mr.
Allworthy has come through with his predictable kindness.

Success in such an undertaking would in all likelihood produce mixed
emotions in any mother caught in similar circumstances. Yet the narrator's
comparison of Bridget's bitter smile to that of one of the Furies is ambiguous. The smile might reflect a higher awareness of things moral in
Bridget than the narrator's characterization of her has granted. She might

"discompose her Features" with a bitter smile because of a profound sense of the painfulness of her own self-inflicted punishment. Because of Allworthy's decision to take the foundling into his household, Bridget is, in fact, condemned to live by her son but not to acknowledge him. The first-time reader, however, is more likely to interpret the comparison between her smile and a Fury's grimace as a sign of self-righteous hypocrisy. Once again the narrator's implications seem to support an initial reading of Bridget's action as that of an aging spinster who transfers her own frustrated sexual drives into self-righteous hostility toward others.

Beyond his comparison of Bridget's smile to that of Tysiphone, the narrator continues his description of Bridget's reaction to her brother's "justice" in the subsequent paragraph:

> With such a Smile then, and with a Voice, sweet as the Evening Breeze of *Boreas* in the pleasant Month of *November*, Miss *Bridget* gently reproved the Curiosity of Mrs. *Deborah*, a Vice with which it seems the latter was too much tainted, and which the former inveighed against with great Bitterness, adding, 'that among all her Faults, she thanked Heaven, her Enemies could not accuse her of prying into the Affairs of other People.' (1: 56)

The narrator's obvious ironic use of *sweet* and *pleasant* serves to underscore the chill of Bridget's character, but the narrator also gains the whole complex of traditional associations connected with winter, such as death, decay, and infertility, with his rhetorical play.[11] Yet, for the reader with a knowledge of Bridget's secret, this passage, like the entire treatment of Bridget by the narrator, becomes richly ironic in a more profound sense than that indicated by the blank assertion that a north wind is "sweet" or that November is "pleasant." Wilkins is dangerous to Bridget, although she was absent, like Mr. Allworthy, during Bridget's pregnancy. Her curiosity could lead her to question Bridget's particular interest in Jenny's case. Wilkins could connect Bridget's previous "sickness" with the sudden appearance of the mysterious infant. Consequently, Bridget's chastisement, which appears to be merely hypocritical on first reading, is highly motivated when read in the light of the cardinal secret of Tom's birth.

The same is true of Bridget's insistence on her own personal lack of culpable "prying into the Affairs of other People." Given the narrator's previous assertion that she often applied herself to the keyhole in the door of her brother's study to overhear his proceedings, the claim appears both ridiculous and hypocritical. But, at least in the particular case of Jenny Jones, Bridget is vitally interested in the proceedings. What happens in the study during the hearing is most assuredly of importance to her and is not only the business of others. The future success of her entire plot may hinge on her knowledge of Jenny's exact evidence. She has, at least, to know if Jenny fulfilled her promise to perjure herself. Also, the use of the word *Affairs* is highly suggestive. Indicative of business in general terms, *Affairs*, of course, might signify a sexual relationship outside of marriage. Complicated by the allusion to the narrator's earlier claim that Bridget's habit of eavesdropping on her brother's cases often gave offense by exposing her to matters "concerning Bastards, and such like" (1: 56), Bridget's statement here carries both possible meanings: she is indeed interested in her own business rather than in the business of others, and that business is sexual in that it is related to her unacknowledged son and, consequently, to her affair with Tom's father, Mr. Summer.

The treatment of Bridget's marriage to Captain Blifil both continues and deepens the narrator's use of such deceptive ambiguity. After being introduced into the household by his brother, Doctor Blifil, and advised of the availability of Miss Bridget, the Captain moves quickly to seal his fortune. Working to suggest a certain perverseness in the relationship, the narrator offers analysis of the contrasting motivation of Bridget and the Captain. Of Bridget's attraction to her gallant, the narrator claims:

> Tho' Miss *Bridget* was a Woman of the greatest
> Delicacy of Taste; yet such were the Charms of the
> Captain's Conversation, that she totally overlooked

the Defects of his Person. She imagined, and perhaps very wisely, that she should enjoy more agreeable Minutes with the Captain, than with a much prettier Fellow; and forewent the Consideration of pleasing her Eyes, in order to procure herself much more solid Satisfaction. (1: 66)

Following a description of the Captain's rugged looks, of his broad shoulders and powerful calves, such a comment on Bridget's "Delicacy of Taste" assumes obvious sexual overtones.

Bridget's delight in "the Charms of the Captain's Conversation" and her wise hopes for "agreeable Minutes with the Captain" both imply sexual intercourse in this ironic context. The double entendre is completed by the last sentence of the paragraph. Here Bridget's rejection of the external "Consideration of pleasing her Eyes" for a "much more solid Satisfaction" carries phallic implications. The narrator's use of the sexually suggestive verb *procure* only reinforces the reading. In fact, the entire travesty of the traditional contrast between external beauty and internal worth, which controls the development of the paragraph, heightens the impression of Bridget's sexual hunger. She takes the Captain, not only because he is the man she can get, but also because she infers from his rugged strength a extraordinary virility.[12]

This reading is supported by the narrator's contrast between Bridget's "love" and that of the giddy young girls that the narrator uses to introduce the chapter:

It hath been observed by wise Men or Women, I forget which, that all Persons are doomed to be in Love once in their Lives. No particular Season is, as I remember, assigned for this; but the Age at which Miss *Bridget* was arrived seems to me as proper a Period as any to be fixed on for this Purpose: It often indeed happens much earlier; but when it doth not, I have observed, it seldom or never fails about this

> Time. Moreover, we may remark that at this Season
> Love is of a more serious and steady Nature than
> what sometimes shews itself in the younger Parts of
> Life. The Love of Girls is uncertain, capricious, and
> so foolish that we cannot always discover what the
> young Lady would be at; nay, it may almost be
> doubted, whether she always knows this herself.
>
>   (1: 64)

Bridget, in short, knows exactly what she desires, unlike a younger woman who might well not completely understand the various complicated social and physical drives that are forcing her toward marriage and mating. The implication is that, while such young Belindas flit through the mating game with all the delightful charms of youth, the older woman drives straight to the main issue. She desires only her "solid Satisfaction."

The narrator's obvious sexual implications indicate that Bridget's attraction to Captain Blifil is purely, even desperately, physical, and such a rhetoric continues to develop Bridget's character as one of an aging virgin whose actions are largely motivated by the drive to procreate. This rhetorical manipulation marks a principal strategy in the narrator's necessary maneuvers to disguise the secret of Tom's birth. Perhaps one could argue that Bridget seems all too knowing in her desire "to procure herself much more solid Satisfaction." Indeed, the announcement that Blifil is born only eight months after the marriage of Bridget and the Captain implies that Bridget is not above a false step in regards to sexual decorum (1: 78). Yet such implications do not really implicate Bridget's previous behavior. In fact, the narrator's use of the commonplace assertion that "all Persons are doomed to be in Love once in their Lives" suggests that this particular instance is Bridget's time, and this implication is reinforced by the narrator's following allusion to her age (1: 64). Furthermore, the narrator's previous revelation that Bridget would often hear "concerning Bastards, and such like" when eavesdropping on her brother's proceedings also helps to explain Bridget's knowledge (1: 56). Both Bridget's knowledge and her premature delivery of Blifil, in other words, can be used to support an initial reading of Bridget's physical attraction to Captain Blifil as being driven by a long history of previous sexual deprivation.

The narrator follows his travesty of the external/internal discourse in Bridget's acceptance of "solid Satisfaction" over physical comeliness with an equally telling description of Captain Blifil's reaction to her "Passion":

> The Captain likewise very wisely preferred the more
> solid Enjoyments he expected with this Lady, to the
> fleeting Charms of Person. He was one of those wise
> Men, who regard Beauty in the other Sex as a very
> worthless and superficial Qualification; or, to speak
> more truly, who rather chuse to possess every Con-
> venience of Life with an ugly Woman, than a hand-
> some one without any of those Conveniences. And
> having a very good Appetite, and but little Nicety, he
> fancied he should play his Part very well at the
> matrimonial Banquet, without the Sauce of Beauty.
>
> (1: 66−67)

Paralleling Bridget's wise choice with the Captain's, the narrator reinforces and sustains his double entendre. Bridget's desire to procure a "more solid Satisfaction" is replaced by the Captain's preference for "the more solid Enjoyments he expected with this Lady." The repetition of the significant adjective *solid* clearly marks the relationship between the two paragraphs, and the substitution of *Enjoyments* for *Satisfaction* appears to make the sexual reading even more tangible, while the modifying phrase "with this Lady" merely furthers the point. Ironically, however, the narrator here returns to the Captain's obvious desire to marry Allworthy's estate in the person of his sister. The Captain is motivated, the narrator remarks, by his desire for "every Convenience of Life"—a fact that the reader knows from the first due to the Captain's introduction into the family by his brother for exactly the possibility of monetary gain through matrimony.

Returning to sexual implications in his concluding sentence of the paragraph, the narrator echoes his own "Bill of Fare" by using eating metaphors. The Captain has "a very good Appetite" but "little Nicety" in his taste. He believes that he will be able to "play his Part very well at the matrimonial Banquet," even "without the Sauce of Beauty." Not only does his appetite lack sophistication and delicacy, but the narrator's metaphorical language implies that it is perverse. His lust is, as it were, directed, not toward the flesh *per se*, but rather toward material wealth and power. Indeed, this implication is supported by the contrast between the Captain, with his "very good Appetite," and those other men the narrator describes in his initial *"fuller Account"* of Bridget who dare not attack the "higher Order of Women" because, as the narrator supposes, they fear a very real lack of "Success" (1: 37).[13]

Through the parallelism of these descriptions of Bridget's desire for "Satisfaction" and the Captain's hope for "solid Enjoyments," as well as through the repetition of key words, the narrator implies that Bridget's violent desire for marriage with the Captain is also something of a corruption of normal sexual drives caused by past deprivation. His discussion of this couple's rejection of physical charms as a "superficial Qualification" travesties the traditional beauty/virtue discourse, for here the "solid" value is sexual gratification on the one hand and material gain on the other. This witty deflation of the traditional distinction between the value of mere external appearance and that of real internal worth points to the serious shortcomings in the character of both Bridget and her Captain. Still, the narrator's treatment of Bridget's motivation in ludicrous sexual terms reinforces the previous description of her as an aging and frustrated maiden.

The narrator's depiction of the actual marriage between Bridget and the Captain in book 2 illustrates their basic hypocrisy and satirizes their Methodist leanings. But this relationship, which degenerates into what the narrator expresses as *"that Felicity which prudent Couples may extract from Hatred,"* ends almost as quickly as it begins (1: 104). After the two years indicated by the narrator in the title to book 2, the Captain's sudden death concludes both the book and the marriage. The narrator's rendering of this particular example of marital *"Felicity"* has served its two major plot functions. It has allowed for the "legitimate," although premature, birth of

Blifil, Tom's main competitor, and it has also misdirected the reader by depicting Bridget as a thoroughly conventional hypocrite, thereby, covering the unconventional intrigue concocted by her and Jenny Jones. Also, in the terms of characterization, this marriage has allowed the narrator to reveal the extremes of Bridget's sexual desire while closely guarding his cardinal secret and, consequently, furthering the deceptive characterization of Bridget necessary to his plot.

Closing his second book with the ironic epitaph for Captain Blifil that was commissioned by Allworthy and written by "a Man of as great Genius as Integrity, and one who perfectly well knew the Captain" (1: 114–15), the narrator skips twelve years to cover the adolescent Tom from age fourteen to nineteen in book 3. After treating Bridget's reaction to her husband's death in the introductory essay, the narrator introduces Tom with a discussion of his youthful vices, beginning with the humorous acknowledgment that Tom "was certainly born to be hanged" (1: 118). Throughout this book, however, the narrator extends his deceptive characterization of Bridget by treating her growing affection for Tom and her fierce dislike, even hatred, for her son, Blifil.

Bridget's initial reaction to her brother's plans to raise the foundling surprised Mrs. Wilkins. The narrator's highly ambiguous statement that Bridget could not have followed her brother's instructions more liberally "had it been a Child of her own" is followed by a series of similar misdirections. In the second book, the narrator had followed the pattern when discussing Allworthy's desire to raise Tom and Blifil together. Of Bridget's reaction, he remarks that "she consented, tho' with some little Reluctance..." (1: 78). He explains Bridget's reluctant consent in the terms of her "great Complacence for her Brother" and then remarks that "she had always behaved towards the Foundling with rather more Kindness than Ladies of rigid Virtue can sometimes bring themselves to shew..." (1: 78–79). Ironically, however, Bridget's reluctance, when read in the light of her actual relation to Tom, becomes, not the apparent reluctance to allow her son, Blifil, to be raised with a bastard, but rather a reluctance to have Tom raised with Blifil. In other words, this reluctance becomes, in the light of the whole truth of Tom's birth, a small hint that Bridget might have had a more honest affection for Mr. Summer and his son than the mutual hate that finally bound her to the Captain and young Blifil.

Nevertheless, in the third book of *Tom Jones*, the narrator indicates that Bridget's public and growing preference for Tom over Blifil is sexual:

> However, when *Tom* grew up, and gave Tokens of that Gallantry of Temper which greatly recommends Men to Women, this Disinclination which she had discovered to him when a Child, by Degrees abated, and at last she so evidently demonstrated her Affection to him to be much stronger than what she bore her own Son, that it was impossible to mistake her any longer. She was so desirous of often seeing him, and discovered such Satisfaction and Delight in his Company, that before he was eighteen Years old, he was become a Rival to both *Square* and *Thwackum*; and what is worse, the whole Country began to talk as loudly of her Inclination to *Tom*, as they had before done of that which she had shewn to *Square*; on which Account the Philosopher conceived the most implacable Hatred for our poor Heroe.
>
> (1: 139–40)

The "Satisfaction and Delight" that Bridget derives from Tom's company, as well as the jealous reactions of Square and Thwackum, all work to create the appearance that Bridget's preference is motivated by sexual desire. By reporting the common gossip without challenge and by noting the difference between Bridget's "Disinclination" for Tom the infant and her "Inclination" toward Tom the young man, the narrator appears to support such a reading.

Ironically, however, this passage foreshadows a number of the major events that will follow Tom's expulsion from Paradise Hall. Since Bridget would be approximately fifty-eight at the time, there is a hint of Tom's later relations with two other older women, Mrs. Waters and Lady Bellaston. Also, for the reader who knows of Bridget's secret, there is a possible indication that Bridget's attraction is incestuous rather than maternal, an attraction that would then humorously foreshadow the incest scare. However, the common gossip about Bridget's preference for Tom over Blifil and the jealous reaction of such characters as Thwackum and Square more likely represent misreadings of Bridget's quite honest maternal affection. The question must remain open. For the first-time reader, nonetheless, the narrator's exploitation of the possibility of Bridget's desire for a May/November relationship between herself and Tom functions as a disguise and furthers his necessary deception.

In the first three books of *Tom Jones*, therefore, the narrator's rhetoric and his treatment of Bridget consistently misdirect the reader. The narrator flattens Bridget into a stock character type, and he exploits the predictable response to the conventional type of the embittered and frustrated spinster. This rhetoric of deceit prevents the first-time reader from discovering the cardinal secret of Tom's birth before the narrator's proper place and time since the narrator can only achieve the particular highly ordered plot that he does achieve in *Tom Jones* by maintaining Bridget's secret. He both places and disguises clues so that the compound ironies of the situation will become apparent after the secret is revealed. But the narrator of *Tom Jones* does not acknowledge the full extent of the mystery about Tom's birth until his own well-planned revelations. To be sure, Tom's father is unknown until Jenny Jones confesses her part in Bridget's plot to Mr. Allworthy. But the identity of Tom's mother appears to be known through most of the text. Jenny had confessed that she was the unwed mother of the infant Tom, and she had accepted Allworthy's punishment. Necessary for the incest scare, Jenny's well-documented sexual adventures as Mrs. Waters appear to substantiate the possibility that Tom did in fact engage in an incestuous relation with his mother at the Upton inn. Indeed, without this further deception, the narrator could not have worked the full complexity of his comic reversal.

Nevertheless, to identify and analyze the narrator's rhetorical misdirection is not to argue that the characterization of Bridget Allworthy in *Tom Jones* represents a serious flaw in Fielding's text. Actually, the conventional and somewhat complacent assertions that Fielding invented the objective, third-person narrator significantly undervalue the comedic achievement of *Tom Jones.* Fielding's masterful achievement is that he has designed a narrative that not only unmasks the villain, Blifil, and rewards the hero, Tom, in the best traditions of comedy, but one that also unmasks the readers, revealing the degree to which conventional assumptions determine the way they read texts. Fielding's narrative engages readers and entraps them. The narrative reveals them to themselves by the rhetorical exploitation of conventional codes of reading. As readers read, they construct meaning from the various signs in the text. They pass judgment on the different characters and the various events of the plot. Like Mr. Allworthy, the readers are assured of their own personal fairness, of their own insight, even of their own mercy and tolerance toward others. The narrator's playful challenges to insensitive readers are not, such readers think, meant for them. They are meant for those other readers who do not possess such a fine understanding. But, once again like Allworthy, the readers learn that they too have been tricked, hoodwinked, deceived into passing judgment with incomplete knowledge of the facts in the case. They learn that the individual human perspective is not an absolute, that sound judgment is always subject to the limitations of human knowledge, and that mercy and tolerance must temper judgment since the human perspective can never be transcendent. Humanity, in short, is limited and human understanding severely circumscribed by humanity's lack of absolute knowledge.

As Tom comes to self-knowledge in the most literal sense in that he learns who his parents were and as Allworthy discovers his own complacency and how he has been tricked by his sister, as well as by the villain, Blifil, so the reader too comes to recognize the limits of personal habits of thought and the more general limits of human intellect through the dramatic interaction with Fielding's deceptive text. Although the whole process is softened by the comic air and the liberties of carnival, the lesson of mercy and tolerance that Tom articulates in the final book of *Tom Jones* is actively supported by the dramatic engagement between the text and its reader, an engagement that teaches self-knowledge through the reader's own inability to predetermine the exact rules of the narrative game.

Notes

1. Samuel Taylor Coleridge, *Specimens of the Table Talk of Samuel Taylor Coleridge*, 2nd ed. (1836; Ann Arbor: University Microfilms, 1967) 310. It is perhaps of some significance that the other two texts that Coleridge praises—*The Alchemist* and *Oedipus Rex*—are a neoclassical comedy dealing with the operations of humorous confidence tricksters and a classical tragedy dealing with judgment. Furthermore, since the plot of *Tom Jones* is in many respects a comic inversion of the plot of *Oedipus*, it should be noted that this classical tragedy deals extensively with incest, vision, and intellectual vanity.

2. Dorothy Van Ghent, *The English Novel: Form and Function* (New York: Holt, 1953) 80 and Frederick W. Hilles, "Art and Artifice in *Tom Jones*," *Imagined Worlds: Essays on Some English Novels and Novelists in Honour of John Butt*, ed. Maynard Mack and Ian Gregor (London: Methuen, 1968) 94.

3. Preston correctly points out that, in his comments upon Bolingbroke's essays, Fielding explicitly rejects analogies between authors and the supreme being as being both improper and impious. Preston further argues that Fielding had a "mistrust of those artists who 'aggrandize their profession with such kind of similies.'" He concludes, therefore, that it may be well not to take Fielding literally in those passages where his narrator appears to make such claims for his own narrative. See John Preston, *The Created Self: The Reader's Role in Eighteenth-Century Fiction* (London: Heinemann, 1970) 99. For Fielding's comments on Bolingbroke quoted by Preston, see Henry Fielding, "A Fragment of a Comment on Lord Bolingbroke's Essays," vol. 16 of *The Complete Works of Henry Fielding, Esq.*, ed. William Ernest Henley (1903; New York: Barnes & Noble, 1967) 314–15.

4. According to Wilbur Cross, all six volumes of the first edition of *Tom Jones* were printed and being advertised by late February 1749. Cross also asserts that Fielding assumed his duties as justice during the winter of 1748–49. See Wilbur L. Cross, *The History of Henry Fielding*, vol. 2 (1918; New York: Russell & Russell, 1963) 117, 223. Consequently, although it would be proper to assume that Fielding may well have been aware of his future post while writing *Tom Jones* and, therefore, considering pertinent themes, it is misleading and inaccurate to think that Fielding wrote *Tom Jones* while he was presiding as a justice.

5. Richard Keller Simon correctly observes that the two most discussed elements of *Tom Jones* have long been the irony of the narrative voice and the complex symmetry of the plot. Complaining that voice and plot are more often than not treated in isolation, Simon insists that critics "must yoke these incongruities together in order to understand the text." His use of the verb *yoke* recalls Dr. Johnson's famous characterization of metaphysical poetry as violently yoking together diverse and contradictory elements. Although one would not wish to brand *Tom Jones* a metaphysical novel, Simon's suggestion does point toward the internal tensions that lurk immediately beneath a facade of Palladian assurance in Fielding's text. Richard Keller Simon, *The Labyrinth of the Comic: Theory and Practice from Fielding to Freud* (Tallahassee: Florida State UP, 1985) 60.

6. Of course, it would be possible for a reader who happened to know the secret of Tom's birth from external sources to read the novel for the first time. But such a reading would be fundamentally different from the reading that proceeded in the dark. It would, in fact, partake of elements of a second reading by shifting the emphasis to how the narrator maintains the secret. John Preston wonders if *Tom Jones* can be read only once or if it must be read more than once. He concludes (and I concur with his conclusion) that it must be read more than once to be understood. See Preston 98.

7. Giving quotations from 1645–1889, the OED defines *Miss* in the first definition listed as "A kept mistress; a concubine. Less commonly, a common prostitute, whore." Definition 2 deals with the more conventional sense: "Prefixed as a title to the name of an unmarried woman or girl (not entitled to the prefix 'Lady' or some higher designation of rank)." The fourth definition adds that when applied to young women or schoolgirls in modern usage there is often a negative connotation of "squeamishness or sentimentality characteristic of girls of such an age." It is possible that similar pejorative associations could apply when used in the context of the conventionalized spinster. See also Samuel Johnson, *Johnson's Dictionary: A Modern Selection*, ed. E. L. McAdam, Jr., and George Milne (New York: Pantheon, 1963) 250. For the inconsistent use of *Miss/Mrs.* in relation to Bridget in the early editions, see Appendix II in the Wesleyan Edition (2: 1012).

8. I am indebted to the editors of the Wesleyan Edition of *Tom Jones* for this detail. I must admit I would not have remembered but for the reminder (1: 35n).

9. Alexander Pope, *Rape of the Lock*, *The Poems of Alexander Pope*, ed. John Butt (New Haven: Yale UP, 1963) 4.4.

10. Joseph Addison, *Spectator* No. 61, *The Spectator*, vol. 1, ed. Donald F. Bond (Oxford: Clarendon, 1965) 259–63.

11. In chapter 11 of the first book, the narrator states that Bridget's likeness may be viewed in Hogarth's "Morning" from *The Four Times of the Day*:

> I would attempt to draw her Picture; but that is done already by a more able Master, Mr. *Hogarth* himself, to whom she sat many Years ago, and hath been lately exhibited by that Gentleman in his Print of a Winter's Morning, of which she was no improper Emblem... (1: 66).

This move, heightened by the sly phrase "many years ago," controls the reader's understanding of Bridget's appearance. Paulson says of this print:

> The lady walking to church, accompanied by her foot-boy who carries her prayer book, is the only person in the scene who does not notice the cold or try to ward it off. It is apparently her element. She pauses to regard (disapprovingly) the group that is composed of Tom King's, the two pairs of lovers, and the lower-class women and the beggar huddled about a fire. All of these people are getting warm in various ways....

See Ronald Paulson, *Hogarth's Graphic Works*, rev. ed., vol. 1 (New Haven: Yale UP, 1970) 179.

12. In the previous paragraph, the narrator has made the contrast between the Captain and young gallants whose bodies have been wrecked by high living:

> In short, his whole Person wanted all that Elegance and Beauty, which is the very reverse of clumsy Strength, and which so agreeably sets off most of our fine Gentlemen; being partly owing to the high Blood of their Ancestors, *viz.* Blood made of rich Sauces and generous Wines, and partly to an early Town Education. (1: 66)

Both the satiric jab at the physical and moral decadence of the "fine Gentlemen" and the implications of gout, venereal disease, and impotence help to support the narrator's suggestions about the Captain's rude vitality.

13. The narrator's figurative relation of love and food also foreshadows his introductory chapter to book 6, "*Of Love.*" His description of the Captain Blifil's appetite parallels his comments about those readers who are incapable of feeling real love. To these he says that "...Love probably may, in your Opinion, very greatly resemble a Dish of Soup, or a Sir-loin of Roast-beef" and that such lean and hungry types are not proper readers for his text (1: 271–72).

CHAPTER 5

Conclusion

It is thought that every activity, artistic or scientific, in fact every deliberate action or pursuit, has for its object the attainment of some good.

Aristotle

The ironic tension established between Fielding's reflexive narrator of *Tom Jones* and the apparent symmetry of the birth-mystery plot that he narrates generates a series of contradictions, subverting the providential implications of the comic resolution. Because of his characteristic intrusiveness, Fielding's narrator becomes visible to the reader as a narrative presence. He becomes a character, an actor, as it were, in the complete action of the narrative. But, by becoming such a character through his intrusive presence, the narrator undermines his own reliability as a disinterested voice speaking from a privileged position. The illusion of a special omniscience is lost, and the narrator's own character and motives acquire importance as data for the interpretative activities of the reader. Through such an ironic loss of the appearance of a transcendent perspective, the narrator's act of narration, his actual story-telling, becomes subject to all of the standard limitations of human discourse. Consequently, one of the most significant elements of the text of *Tom Jones* is the narrator's rhetoric, his various narrative selections and semantic moves designed to control and direct the reader's response to the actions and characters that he depicts. Given the comic birth-mystery plot, the structure that controls the development of the text is the narrator's strategic withholding of pertinent information since the narrator is obligated to disguise Tom's true identity and the exact circumstances surrounding his birth so that he will be able to reveal them at the proper time to achieve the comic resolution and to create the appearance of the hidden workings of a special providence.

The narrator's characteristic withholding of vital information is coupled to an active rhetoric of misdirection and deception. Particularly operative in the characterization of Bridget Allworthy, the narrator's deception ironically parallels the various hypocrisies practiced by Blifil and the scheme Bridget and Jenny Jones concoct to trick Allworthy into adopting Tom. The degree to which the reflexive narrative method foregrounds the narrator as narrator and emphasizes the *told* quality of the text, however, indicates that the reader should recognize that the narrator must become a hypocrite himself to reveal the hypocrisy of the characters. Yet, in the comic world of *Tom Jones*, this paradox does not brand the narrator a villain but rather merely a comic rogue. His position is paradoxical because, while he must deceive the reader to complete his plot, the final result of the narrator's deception is the comic unmasking of the reader's own intellectual and ethical shortcomings—an end that is benevolent in that it leads to an increase in the reader's self-knowledge, as well as to an experience that illustrates the necessity of tolerance and intellectual prudence. Consequently, the narrator of *Tom Jones* is best read as something other than either an unambiguous representative of a benevolent providence working toward some unseen good or a vicious Machiavellian driving for power over the reader through an undue insistence on how the text should be understood. Rather, it would seem that the narrator of *Tom Jones* is best understood as a complex comic figure whose devious play with his readers, coupled with his thematic insistence on the necessity of tolerance and mercy, forces the reader toward a shock of recognition that dramatically illustrates all of the serious limitations of human understanding brought on by the lack of absolute knowledge.

The narrator's intrusiveness, his continual commentary on the action, and his discussions of his own narrative practices all indicate that his deceptive rhetoric is ultimately to be discovered by the reader. Certainly, Fielding designed much of his narrator's deceptive play with conventional comic structures to be recognized by his readers. As R. S. Crane asserts, although the plot of *Tom Jones* produces "a kind of faint alarm which is the comic analogue of fear," this feeling does not develop "in any positive degree" because of an awareness that Tom's "mistakes will not issue in any permanent frustration of our wishes for his good."[1] Indeed, the narrator plays with the potential for tragedy that is always an element of comic plots when, for example, he insists that Tom "was certainly born to be hanged" (1: 118). Additionally, the narrator extends this play with the conventional expectations of comedy when, in chapter 1, book 17, he refuses to aid Tom with any "supernatural Assistance" (2: 875–76), claiming that he would rather Tom "was hanged at *Tyburn*" than that he should "shock the Faith of our Reader" with the use of any such device as *deus ex machina* to save his hero from the gallows and bring about the happy ending (2: 876).

The comic point of such play with the convention of sudden and surprising reversals inherent in comedy is predicated on the reader's awareness that the text is a comic one. Ironically, however, these playful intrusions by the narrator only help to reinforce the narrator's visibility as a narrator. As the narrator teases the reader's expectations raised by the general comic tone of the text, the reader's attention is shifted from the mere suspense of the story to the workings of the plot. The narrator's intrusions and his playful mocking of comic expectations emphasize how he tells Tom's story at the expense of the raw material of the story itself. Expecting the traditional comic turn and happy resolution, the reader's attention is drawn to how the narrator ties and then cuts his complicated knot, is drawn, in short, to the narrator's own narrative act.

The narrator himself graphically illustrates this point when he directs the reader to return to the text in the light of the new information being released during the climactic chapters. Immediately after Partridge has, with suitable shock and dismay, revealed to Tom that Jenny Jones and Mrs. Waters are one and the same person and Tom has registered his Oedipal horror—"O good heavens! Incest—with a Mother!" (2: 915–16), the narrator invites the reader to return to the scenes at Upton and to examine the subtle workings of circumstance:

> If the Reader will please to refresh his Memory, by
> turning to the Scene at Upton in the Ninth Book, he
> will be apt to admire the many strange Accidents
> which unfortunately prevented any Interview between
> Partridge and Mrs. *Waters*, when she spent a whole
> Day there with Mr. *Jones*. Instances of this Kind we
> may frequently observe in Life, where the greatest
> events are produced by a nice Train of little Cir-
> cumstances; and more than one Example of this may
> be discovered by the accurate Eye, in this our His-
> tory. (2: 916)

The narrator here directs the reader to return to the text and to note the various devious manipulations that he has worked. Particularly true of the final clause, the narrator's direction indicates that, besides the Jenny Jones/Mrs. Waters convolution, there will be other examples in the text for "the accurate Eye" to discover.

Although the narrator directs the reader to discover the previous manipulation, the final irony is that the narrator can only make the need for such discoveries evident to the reader by having hidden the information in the first place. For all of his self-revealing intrusiveness, his apparent openness and alleged reliability, the narrator can only achieve his orderly "Palladian" plot by carefully withholding pertinent information from the reader for much of the text. This strategic withholding, as well as the accompanying deception illustrated by the characterization of Bridget, functions on both the macro and the micro levels. Under, as it were, the overarching structure of the birth-mystery plot, the narrator continually misleads the reader in scene after scene, slowly giving corrective information only after he has established initial, misleading assertions.

An example of this tactic is the involved method the narrator employs to reveal that the barber Little Benjamin is indeed Partridge, Tom's nominal father. In chapter 4, book 8, after he has been wounded by Northerton, Tom meets Little Benjamin in the character of a barber. The narrator introduces Benjamin as a comic character, comparing him to the Barber of

Baghdad and Cervantes's Nicholas (1: 413). Describing this barber as an "extraordinary Person," the narrator states that Little Benjamin "was a Fellow of great Oddity and Humour, which had frequently led him into small Inconveniencies, such as Slaps in the Face, Kicks in the Breech, broken Bones, &c" (1: 414). However, in chapter 6, book 8, the narrator reveals that, in addition to being a comical barber, Little Benjamin also possesses some very real medical skills that he applies to Tom's wounds (1: 422–23). Finding the skills of barber and surgeon in the same individual was not unusual in the eighteenth century. Nevertheless, the narrator allows the reader to formulate an interpretation of the character, and then he slowly leaks information that forces revision.

The same deceptive pattern is followed with the name *Little Benjamin* itself. At first, a reader might well assume that the adjective *little* is to be taken literally. Perhaps a more sophisticated reader would recognize a humorous Aristotelian allusion to Benjamin's stature as a comic character. But, after it has been revealed that Little Benjamin is in fact Partridge, the narrator begins chapter 8, book 8, by forcing the reader to revise any such view by adding information that he has previously withheld:

> Mr. *Jones*, and *Partridge*, or *Little Benjamin*, (which Epithet of *Little* was perhaps given him ironically, he being in reality near six Feet high) having left their last Quarters in the Manner before described, travelled on to *Gloucester* without meeting any Adventure worth relating. (1: 430)

The parenthetical statement reveals that Little Benjamin is not only not really Little Benjamin but that he is not even really little. The *little* is ironic, and any conception of Little Benjamin that the reader might have formed now has to be revised and integrated with the understanding of Partridge drawn from the information given in earlier books.

Such a process of interpretative revision is both complicated and enriched by Partridge's humorous acting out of his various roles of barber and surgeon in the person of Little Benjamin. After his insistence that a surgeon must have "a grave Aspect" while "A Barber may make you laugh," Partridge interrupts Tom's facetious reply and laments the separation of his various roles:

> 'Mr. *Barber*, or Mr. *Surgeon*, or Mr. *Barber-Surgeon*,'
> said *Jones*.—'O dear Sir,' answered *Benjamin*, inter-
> rupting him, '*Infandum Regina jubes renovare Dolorem*.
> You recal to my Mind that cruel Separation of the
> united Fraternities, so much to the Prejudice of both
> Bodies, as all Separations must be, according to the
> old Adage, *Vis unita fortior*; which to be sure there
> are not wanting some of one or of the other Frater-
> nity who are able to construe. What a Blow was this
> to me who unite both in my own Person.'—'Well, by
> whatever Name you please to be called,' continued
> *Jones*, 'you certainly are one of the oddest, most
> comical Fellows I ever met with, and must have
> something very surprizing in your Story, which you
> must confess I have a Right to hear.' (1: 423–24)

By lamenting the split between barbers and surgeons, Partridge humorously indicates the fracture in his own life between the identity of Partridge and that of Little Benjamin. Tom, of course, has the right to hear Partridge's story because he has told him his, but the reader soon learns that he has a more fundamental justification because, throughout his life, Tom has been led to believe that Partridge is his father.

The point, however, is that the elements of the Little Benjamin scenes exactly reproduce in miniature the overall scheme of the birth-mystery plot. The narrator initially offers partial information and then slowly releases additional facts that complicate the issue and force the readers toward a continual revision of their understanding of the text. To be sure, this process functions to a certain degree in any extended fiction, but Fielding's use of an intrusive narrator and the constant reference to the methods and modes of composition indicate that such a process is of considerable importance to an understanding of *Tom Jones*. Calling attention to himself by his intrusions into the text, the narrator uses his apparent openness to help disguise his deception so that he can complete his plot; nevertheless, at the same time, the various discussions of his narrative selection, his directions to the reader, and the entire host of comments and commentary he offers on reading, writing, and criticism, as well as other aspects of the narrative act, all foreground the act of narration, making narrative itself the subject of the text.

Exploring the textuality of narrative is a recurring aspect of Fielding's fiction. *Joseph Andrews*, like *Tom Jones*, is constructed around mistaken identity and a birth-mystery, but deception is not a principal device in this lighter, more jovial text. The narrator of *Joseph Andrews* knows how his plot will be resolved because he is telling a retrospective narrative, but, because Mrs. Andrews, who knows that Joseph is a changeling, is not present until the climax, the narrator does not actively deceive the reader about her knowledge or character as the narrator of *Tom Jones* does with his characterization of Bridget Allworthy. The narrator of *Joseph Andrews* gathers the various characters together on the Booby country estate and allows the discovery of Joseph's origin to be made and the incest question to be resolved through the catalyst of the gypsy. Although the narrator withholds important information from the reader throughout most of the narrative, he is not obliged by his plot to practice the sustained deception that the narrator of *Tom Jones* must actively pursue.

Nevertheless, *Joseph Andrews* is structured around the principle of the timely revelation of strategically withheld information. In a scene that parallels the Little Benjamin episode in *Tom Jones*, Parson Adams's identity is obscured when he enters the Tow-wouse inn where Joseph is recovering from the wounds received when he was robbed and beaten:

> It was now the Dusk of the Evening, when a grave
> Person rode into the Inn, and committing his Horse
> to the Hostler, went directly into the Kitchin, and
> having called for a Pipe of Tobacco, took his place
> by the Fire-side; where several other Persons were
> likewise assembled.[2]

Only after several pages does the narrator reveal Parson Adams's identity:

> He was accordingly conducted up by *Betty*: but what,
> Reader, was the surprize on both sides, when he saw
> *Joseph* was the Person in Bed; and when *Joseph*
> discovered the Face of his good Friend Mr. *Abraham*
> *Adams.*[3]

This episode, therefore, represents an early working of the more developed sequence in *Tom Jones*. As in the case of the Little Benjamin/Partridge episode, an important character is reintroduced as if he were a completely new one, and, after the belated revelation of his identity, that character becomes the travelling companion of the hero.

A second example of the narrator's exploitation of strategic withholding in *Joseph Andrews* comes from the joint where the initial parody of Richardson's *Pamela* opens into the more extensive comedy of the road. Joseph is originally presented as a rather narrow and even priggish young footman who rejects Lady Booby's sexual advances because of an abstract notion of virtue modeled on the famous example of Pamela. Indeed, such a characterization is actually necessitated by the parodic intent. Revealing the hypocrisy and vanity implicit in the Richardsonian method of first-person, epistolary narration, the narrator records two letters that Joseph writes to Pamela reporting on Lady Booby's advances and his precarious situation in London.

In his first letter, Joseph reports to Pamela of Lady Booby's suggestive actions, while repeatedly remarking on his dislike of servants revealing the secrets of the family:

> Don't tell any body what I write, because I should
> not care to have Folks say I discover what passes in
> our Family; but if it had not been so great a Lady, I
> should have thought she had had a mind to me.
> Dear *Pamela*, don't tell any body: but she ordered
> me to sit down by her Bed-side, when she was in
> naked Bed [sic]; and she held my Hand, and talked

exactly as a Lady does to her Sweetheart in a Stage-Play, which I have seen in *Covent-Garden*, while she wanted him to be no better than he should be.[4]

Although Joseph reveals several unpleasant characteristics in this letter, the real parodic point is directed at the limits of Richardson's theory of morality and his narrative method.

In his second letter, however, Joseph shows a spark of real human warmth when he admits to Pamela that he has in fact been sorely tempted: "But I am glad she turned me out of the Chamber as she did: for I had once almost forgotten every word Parson *Adams* had ever said to me."[5] For his part, the narrator quickly follows this hint in Joseph's letter with the announcement that he has withheld a secret "the Reader, without being a Conjurer, cannot possibly guess; 'till we have given him those hints, which it may be now proper to open."[6] His next chapter, "*Of several new Matters not expected*," reveals that "there lived a young Girl whom *Joseph* (tho' the best of Sons and Brothers) longed more impatiently to see than his Parents or his Sister."[7] Joseph, it appears, has other reasons for rejecting Lady Booby's advances than his desire to imitate Pamela's success with Mr. B.

Still, the narrator's introduction of Joseph's sincere affection for Fanny Goodwill forces readers first to hang fire and then to revise their previous reading of both Joseph's character and the motivation for his rejection of Lady Booby's offers. The narrow, unpleasant, and hypocritical Joseph of the initial parody who tells of Lady Booby's behavior while exclaiming his dislike of common gossip develops into a more vital comic figure whose virtue is an act of affirmation, not merely one of negation. Joseph no longer appears to be a manikin who ludicrously reproduces Pamela's self-righteous virtue. With the additional knowledge of his love for Fanny, Joseph's rejection of Lady Booby's advances takes on new shape and shadings, assuming some of the implications of the latitudinarian position so often preached by Parson Adams that good works and not only faith lead to salvation.

Significantly, both of these examples from *Joseph Andrews* illustrate the link between the narrator's use of withholding and his intrusive emphasis on the processes of reading and writing. During his comic reintroduction of Adams as "a grave Person," the narrator simply makes one intrusive address to the reader that marks both Joseph's and the reader's surprise.[8] In the more extended introduction of Joseph's love for his illiterate country lass, Fanny, however, the narrator employs all of the elaborate machinery of humorous chapter endings, telling chapter titles, and the explicit linking of his method to sudden revelation and surprise. In fact, the narrator claims that his book is not a simple one but rather one "where the Scene opens itself by small degrees, and he is a sagacious Reader who can see two Chapters before him."[9] Clearly indicative of further surprise, such a statement of principle also indicates the degree to which the actual process of reading is placed in the foreground as an element of the explicit play of the text.

A similar interest in the narrative act itself can be seen in the other extended fictions in Fielding's canon, with the notable exception of his one major failure, *Amelia*. The minor *A Journey from This World to the Next* is built upon all of the old quixotic mechanics of lost-and-found manuscripts, illegible script, and editorial presentation. *Shamela*, of course, parodies Richardson's moral theory and his first-person, epistolary narrative method, as well as Cibber's tortured style and arrogance. *Jonathan Wild* foregrounds the narrative act in the long romance narration of Mrs. Heartfree by exploiting the ironic tensions between her role as the ideal wife and her actions as a narrator. In *Amelia*, on the other hand, Fielding maintains much of his characteristic narrative machinery of intrusion and commentary, but the tone of the complex comic voice has faded. The intrusive narrator of this text is neither fully integrated into nor supportive of the social purpose expressed in the theme. Even the comic resolution that leaves Amelia and Booth happy and secure seems forced and only vaguely shadows the more successful comic resolutions of *Joseph Andrews* and *Tom Jones*. Losing his characteristic play with the narrative act in his social purpose, Fielding fails in *Amelia* to create the paradoxical narrative voice whose ironic convolution is the hallmark of his two comic successes.

In *Joseph Andrews* and *Tom Jones*, however, Fielding maintains a precarious balance. The lighter, more jovial *Joseph Andrews* is, no doubt, largely the dress-rehearsal for its more complex successor. As in *Tom Jones*, the narrator withholds important information to allow for the sudden reversal of circumstances at the appropriate time, but the narrator of *Joseph Andrews* is not obliged to institute the whole complex of deceptive rhetoric that the narrator of *Tom Jones* is forced to engage in because of the difference in the design of the plot. In *Joseph Andrews*, the narrator assembles his characters on the Booby estate and allows for the discovery of the secret of Joseph's birth. In *Tom Jones*, the narrator furthers his withholding of pertinent information by his misleading characterization of Bridget Allworthy. This foregrounding of deception darkens *Tom Jones* and transforms the familiar techniques of comic romance into the maneuvers of ironic comedy.

The narrator's constant employment of a controlled release of information and his sophistic trickery engage readers with the text, compelling them to revise previous conceptions and interpretations. Such a process emphasizes the reader's limitations of judgment, forcing the realization that, like Mr. Allworthy, readers might well be complacent in their intellectual abilities. This textual process neatly meshes with the themes of prudence, tolerance, and mercy that are principal themes in the discourse. Indeed, the intrusive narrative method reproduces in all of its ironic tensions Fielding's lifelong insistence that the letter of any law must be enlivened by a prudent reading that allows for a warm and good-hearted expression of the spirit.

Notes

1. R. S. Crane, "The Plot of *Tom Jones*," *Journal of General Education* 4 (1950): 126.

2. Henry Fielding, *Joseph Andrews*, ed. Martin C. Battestin, *The Wesleyan Edition of the Works of Henry Fielding*, ex. ed. W. B. Coley (Middletown: Wesleyan UP, 1967) 61.

3. Henry Fielding, *Joseph Andrews* 61.

4. Henry Fielding, *Joseph Andrews* 31.

5. Henry Fielding, *Joseph Andrews* 46–47.

6. Henry Fielding, *Joseph Andrews* 47.

7. Henry Fielding, *Joseph Andrews* 48.

8. Henry Fielding, *Joseph Andrews* 64.

9. Henry Fielding, *Joseph Andrews* 48.

Bibliography

Abrams, M. H. *The Mirror and the Lamp: Romantic Theory and the Critical Tradition*. London: Oxford UP, 1953.

Addison, Joseph. *Spectator* No. 61. *The Spectator*. Vol. 1. Ed. Donald F. Bond. Oxford: Clarendon, 1965. 259–63.

Alter, Robert. *Fielding and the Nature of the Novel*. Cambridge: Harvard UP, 1968.

——————. *Partial Magic: The Novel as a Self-Conscious Genre*. Berkeley: U of California P, 1975.

Aristotle. *De Poetica*. Trans. Ingram Bywater. Vol. 11. *The Works of Aristotle*. Ed. W. D. Ross. Oxford: Clarendon, 1959. 1447a–1462b.

——————. *The Ethics of Aristotle*. Trans. J. A. K. Thomson. London: George Allen & Unwin, 1953.

Auerbach, Erich. *Mimesis: The Representation of Reality in Western Literature*. Trans. Willard R. Trask. Princeton: Princeton UP, 1953.

Bakhtin, M. M. *The Dialogic Imagination: Four Essays by M. M. Bakhtin*. Trans. Caryl Emerson and Michael Holquist. Ed. Michael Holquist. Austin: U of Texas P, 1981.

——————. *Rabelais and His World*. Trans. Helene Iswolsky. Cambridge: MIT P, 1968.

Battestin, Martin C. Introduction. *Joseph Andrews and Shamela*. Ed. Martin C. Battestin. London: Methuen, 1965. v–xl.

——————. *The Moral Basis of Fielding's Art: A Study of* Joseph Andrews. Middleton: Wesleyan UP, 1959.

——————. *The Providence of Wit: Aspects of Form in Augustan Literature and the Arts*. Oxford: Clarendon, 1974.

Battestin, Martin C., and Ruthe R. Battestin. *Henry Fielding: A Life*. London: Routledge, 1989.

Blanchard, Frederic T. *Fielding the Novelist: A Study in Historical Criticism*. New Haven: Yale UP, 1926.

Booth, Wayne C. *The Rhetoric of Fiction*. 2nd ed. Chicago: U of Chicago P, 1983.

——————. *A Rhetoric of Irony*. Chicago: U of Chicago P, 1975.

Boswell, James. *Boswell's Life of Johnson*. London: Oxford UP, 1953.

Chaucer, Geoffrey. *The Canterbury Tales*. *The Works of Geoffrey Chaucer*. Ed. F. N. Robinson. 2nd ed. Boston: Houghton, 1957. 17–265.

Coleridge, Samuel Taylor. *Specimens of the Table Talk of Samuel Taylor Coleridge*. 2nd ed. 1836. Ann Arbor: University Microfilms, 1967.

Cornford, Francis Macdonald. *The Origin of Attic Comedy*. Gloucester: Peter Smith, 1968.

Coventry, Francis. Dedication. *The History of Pompey the Little or The Life and Adventures of a Lap-dog*. Ed. Robert Adams Day. London: Oxford UP, 1974. xli-xlv.

Crane, R. S. "The Plot of *Tom Jones*." *Journal of General Education* 4 (1950): 112–30.

Cross, Wilbur L. *The History of Henry Fielding.* 3 vols. 1918. New York: Russell & Russell, 1963.

Dennis, John. The Epistle Dedicatory. *The Advancement and Reformation of Modern Poetry.* Vol. 1. *The Critical Works of John Dennis.* Ed. Edward Niles Hooker. Baltimore: Johns Hopkins P, 1939. 197–207.

Dudden, F. Homes. *Henry Fielding: His Life, Works, and Times.* 2 vols. Hamden: Archon, 1966.

Eagleton, Terry. *Literary Theory: An Introduction.* Minneapolis: U of Minnesota P, 1983.

Empson, William. "*Tom Jones.*" *Fielding: A Collection of Critical Essays.* Ed. Ronald Paulson. Englewood Cliffs: Prentice-Hall, 1962.

Fielding, Henry. *Amelia.* Vols. 6–7 of Henley, *Complete Works.*

———. *An Apology for the Life of Mrs. Shamela Andrews.* Ed. Sheridan W. Baker, Jr. Berkeley: U of California P, 1953.

———. "Articles in the Champion." Vol. 15 of Henley, *Complete Works* 75–338.

———. *The Covent-Garden Journal.* 2 vols. Ed. Gerard Edward Jensen. New York: Russell & Russell, 1964.

———. "A Fragment of a Comment on Lord Bolingbroke's Essays." Vol. 16 of Henley, *Complete Works* 311–22.

———. *The History of the Adventures of Joseph Andrews and His Friend Mr. Abraham Adams.* New York: Norton, 1958.

———. *The History of the Life of the Late Mr. Jonathan Wild.* Vol. 2 of Henley, *Complete Works* 1–207.

———. *The History of Tom Jones: A Foundling.* Ed. Fredson Bowers. 2 vols. Oxford: Wesleyan UP, 1975. *The Wesleyan Edition of the Works of Henry Fielding.* Ex. ed. W. B. Coley.

———. *The History of Tom Jones: A Foundling.* New York: Random, 1950.

———. *Joseph Andrews.* Ed. Martin C. Battestin. Middletown: Wesleyan UP, 1967. *The Wesleyan Edition of the Works of Henry Fielding.* Ex. ed. W. B. Coley.

———. *The Journal of a Voyage to Lisbon, by the Late Henry Fielding, Esq.* Ed. Austin Dobson. Vol. 16 of Henley, *Complete Works* 168–308.

———. *A Journey from This World to the Next.* London: Dent, 1973.

———. *A Journey from This World to the Next, &c.* Vol. 2 of Henley, *Complete Works* 209–343.

———. *The Life of Mr. Jonathan Wild the Great.* 1962. New York: New American Library, 1982.

———. "The Lottery, A Farce." Vol. 8 of Henley, *Complete Works* 265–98.

———. *The Tragedy of Tragedies; or, The Life and Death of Tom Thumb the Great.* Vol. 9 of Henley, *Complete Works* 5–72.

Ford, Ford Madox. *Critical Writings of Ford Madox Ford.* Ed. Frank MacShane. Regents Critics Series. Gen. ed. Paul A. Olson. Lincoln: U of Nebraska P, 1964.

Forster, E. M. *Aspects of the Novel.* New York: Harvest, 1955.

Foster, Dennis A. *Confession and complicity in narrative.* Cambridge: Cambridge UP, 1987.

Frye, Northrop. *Anatomy of Criticism: Four Essays.* Princeton: Princeton UP, 1957.

Hahn, H. George, and Carl Behm III. *The Eighteenth-Century British Novel and Its*

Background: An Annotated Bibliography and Guide to Topics. London: Scarecrow, 1985.

Harrison, Bernard. *Henry Fielding's* Tom Jones: *The Novelist as Moral Philosopher*. London: Sussex UP, 1975.

Hatfield, Glenn W. *Henry Fielding and the Language of Irony*. Chicago: U of Chicago P, 1968.

Henley, William Ernest, ed. *The Complete Works of Henry Fielding, Esq.* By Henry Fielding. 16 vols. 1903. New York: Barnes & Noble, 1967.

Heraclitus. Fragment 231. *The Presocratic Philosophers: A Critical History with a Selection of Texts*. Ed. G. S. Kirk and J. E. Raven. Cambridge: Cambridge UP, 1971. 204.

Hilles, Frederick W. "Art and Artifice in *Tom Jones*." *Imagined Worlds: Essays on Some English Novels and Novelists in Honour of John Butt*. Ed. Maynard Mack and Ian Gregor. London: Methuen, 1968. 91–110.

Hume, David. *An Inquiry Concerning Human Understanding*. Ed. Charles W. Hendel. 1955. New York: Liberal Arts P, 1957.

Hutchens, Eleanor Newman. *Irony in* Tom Jones. University: U of Alabama P, 1965.

Irwin, Michael. *Henry Fielding: The Tentative Realist*. Oxford: Clarendon, 1967.

Irwin, William Robert. *The Making of* Jonathan Wild: *A Study in the Literary Method of Henry Fielding*. Hamden: Archon, 1966.

Iser, Wolfgang. *The Act of Reading: A Theory of Aesthetic Response*. Baltimore: Johns Hopkins UP, 1978.

——————. *The Implied Reader: Patterns of Communication in Prose Fiction from Bunyan to Beckett*. Baltimore: Johns Hopkins UP, 1974.

James, Henry. *The Art of the Novel*. New York: Scribner's, 1962.

Jefferson, Ann, and David Robey, eds. *Modern Literary Theory: A Comparative Introduction*. Totowa: Barnes & Noble, 1982.

Johnson, Samuel. *The History of Rasselas, Prince of Abissinia*. Ed. J. P. Hardy. 1968. Oxford: Oxford UP, 1990.

——————. *Johnson's Dictionary: A Modern Selection*. Ed. E. L. McAdam, Jr., and George Milne. New York: Pantheon, 1963.

——————. Preface to Shakespeare, 1765. *Johnson on Shakespeare*. Ed. Arthur Sherbo. Vol. 7. *The Yale Edition of the Works of Samuel Johnson*. New Haven: Yale UP, 1968.

——————. *Rambler* No. 4. *The Rambler*. Vol. 3. *The Yale Edition of the Works of Samuel Johnson*. Ed. W. J. Bate and Albrecht B. Strauss. New Haven: Yale UP, 1969. 19–25.

Kennedy, George A. *Classical Rhetoric and Its Christian and Secular Tradition from Ancient to Modern Times*. Chapel Hill: U of North Carolina P, 1980.

Kinkead-Weeks, Mark. "Out of the Thicket in *Tom Jones*." *Henry Fielding: Justice Observed*. Ed. K. G. Simpson. London: Vision, 1985. 137–57.

Livy. *The War with Hannibal: Books XXI–XXX of* The History of Rome from Its Foundation. Trans. Aubrey de Sélincourt. Ed. Betty Radice. London: Penguin, 1965.

Locke, John. *An Essay Concerning Human Understanding*. Ed. Alexander Campbell Fraser. 2 vols. Oxford: Clarendon, 1894.

Lockwood, Thomas. "Matter and Reflection in *Tom Jones*." *ELH: A Journal of English History* 45 (1978): 226–35.

McKeon, Michael. *The Origins of the English Novel, 1600–1740.* Baltimore: Johns Hopkins UP, 1987.

McLynn, Frank. *Crime and Punishment in Eighteenth-century England.* 1989. Oxford: Oxford UP, 1991.

Miller, Henry Knight. *Henry Fielding's* Tom Jones *and the Romance Tradition.* English Literary Studies 6. Victoria: U of Victoria, 1976.

——————. "The Voices of Henry Fielding: Style in *Tom Jones.*" *The Augustan Milieu: Essays Presented to Louis A. Landa.* Ed. Henry Knight Miller, Eric Rothstein, and G. S. Rousseau. Oxford: Clarendon, 1970. 262–88.

Monboddo, James Burnett, Lord. *Of the Origin and Progress of Language.* 3 vols. Edinburgh, 1776.

Paulson, Ronald. *Hogarth's Graphic Works.* Rev. ed. 2 vols. New Haven: Yale UP, 1970.

——————. Introduction. *Fielding: A Collection of Critical Essays.* Ed. Ronald Paulson. Englewood Cliffs: Prentice-Hall, 1962. 1–11.

Paulson, Ronald, and Thomas Lockwood. *Henry Fielding: The Critical Heritage.* London: Routledge and Kegan Paul, 1969.

Plato. *Gorgias.* Trans. Terence Irwin. Oxford: Clarendon, 1979.

Pope, Alexander. *Peri Bathous: or, Martinus Scriblerus, His Treatise of the Art of Sinking in Poetry.* Ed. Rosemary Cowler. Vol. 2. *The Prose Works of Alexander Pope.* Hamden: Archon, 1986. 171–276.

——————. *The Rape of the Lock.* *The Poems of Alexander Pope.* Ed. John Butt. New Haven: Yale UP, 1963. 217–42.

Preston, John. *The Created Self: The Reader's Role in Eighteenth-Century Fiction.* London: Heinemann, 1970.

Rawson, C. J. *Henry Fielding and the Augustan Ideal Under Stress.* London: Routledge and Kegan Paul, 1972.

Richardson, Samuel. *The Selected Letters of Samuel Richardson.* Ed. John Carroll. Oxford: Clarendon, 1964.

Rogers, Pat. *Henry Fielding: A Biography.* New York: Scribner's, 1979.

Rothstein, Eric. "Virtues of Authority in *Tom Jones.*" *The Eighteenth Century: Theory and Interpretation* 28 (1987): 99–126.

Scholes, Robert. *Semiotics and Interpretation.* New Haven: Yale UP, 1982.

Scott, Sir Walter. *Sir Walter Scott: On Novelists and Fiction.* Ed. Ioan Williams. New York: Barnes & Noble, 1968.

Shaftesbury, Anthony, Earl of. *Characteristics of Men, Manners, Opinions, Times, etc.* Ed. John M. Robertson. 2 vols. 1900. Gloucester: Peter Smith, 1963.

Shklovsky, Victor. "Sterne's *Tristram Shandy*: Stylistic Commentary." *Russian Formalist Criticism: Four Essays.* Trans. Lee T. Lemon and Marion J. Reis. Regents Critics Series. Gen. ed. Paul A. Olson. Lincoln: U of Nebraska P, 1965.

Simon, Richard Keller. *The Labyrinth of the Comic: Theory and Practice from Fielding to Freud.* Tallahassee: Florida State UP, 1985.

Smith, Barbara Herrnstein. "Narrative Versions, Narrative Theories." *On Narrative.* Ed. W. J. T. Mitchell. Chicago: U of Chicago P, 1981. 209–32.

Stamper, Rex. "The Narrator of *Tom Jones*: Traditional and Modern Readers." *Publications of the Mississippi Philological Association* 1989: 197–206.

Thucydides. *The History of the Peloponnesian War*. Trans. Rex Warner. Penguin, 1954.

Todorov, Tzvetan. *Genres in Discourse*. Trans. Catherine Porter. Cambridge: Cambridge UP, 1990.

——————. *The Poetics of Prose*. Trans. Richard Howard. Ithaca: Cornell UP, 1977.

Van Ghent, Dorothy. *The English Novel: Form and Function*. New York: Holt, 1953.

Watt, Ian. *The Rise of the Novel: Studies in Defoe, Richardson, and Fielding*. Berkeley: U of California P, 1957.

Wright, Andrew. *Henry Fielding: Mask and Feast*. Berkeley: U of California P, 1965.

Index